Did you read this book - Leave your mark

WHY WORRY?

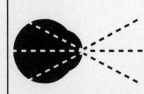

This Large Print Book carries the
Seal of Approval of N.A.V.H.

WHY WORRY?

STOP COPING AND START LIVING

KATHRYN TRISTAN

THORNDIKE PRESS

A part of Gale, Cengage Learning

Detroit • New York • San Francisco • New Haven, Conn • Waterville, Maine • London

LIBRARY OF CONGRESS CATALOGING-IN-PUBLICATION DATA

Tristan, Kathryn.
    Why worry? : stop coping and start living / by Kathryn Tristan. — Large print edition.
        pages cm. — (Thorndike Press large print health, home & learning)
    Originally published as: Anxiety rescue (Chesterfield, MO : Dancing Eagle Press, c2007).
    Includes bibliographical references.
    ISBN-13: 978-1-4104-5726-4 (hardcover)
    ISBN-10: 1-4104-5726-5 (hardcover)
    1. Anxiety—Prevention. 2. Worry—Prevention. 3. Fear—Prevention. I. Tristan, Kathryn. Anxiety rescue. II. Title.
    RC531.T755 2013
    616.85'22—dc23   2012050723

Published in 2013 by arrangement with Atria, a division of Simon & Schuster, Inc.

CONTENTS

CORE CONCEPT 2: I CHOOSE TO CHANGE MY OUTLOOK

INTRODUCTION:
HOW THIS BOOK
CAN HELP YOU

That the birds of worry and care fly over
your head, this you cannot change, but
that they build nests in your hair,
this you can prevent.
— Chinese proverb

We all worry. It's a natural part of living. A biologically built-in mechanism, worry was designed to help us. Where do we go wrong? For millions worldwide, worries are eating away at our sense of security and our feelings of well-being, and are ultimately downsizing our happiness while supersizing our stress. We cannot open a newspaper, turn on the television, listen to the radio, or surf the internet without witnessing chaos, catastrophes, or just plain old bad news.

Our personal lives also are challenged. Work, home, relationships, finances, health: each aspect is one ball in our juggling act. Keeping them all in the air while balancing

9

emails, voicemails, and unending responsibilities creates mounting tension that can keep us stressed, worried, and tense. What will happen next?

The real question is, how can we use this natural reaction and harness it to "worry smart" rather than letting worry control our lives? How can we use it to arm rather than to harm? *Why Worry?* tackles this issue head-on and shows in simple language, using easy strategies, how to do just that.

Worry is a multifaceted emotion with many forms and intensities. In its simplest understanding, worry is a response to a stressful situation that is fueled by analysis, imagination, and often exaggeration. Depending on your responses and the mix of these three elements, worry may help you solve a problem or overwhelm you with fears about future calamities.

Worry is the hub, the nucleus, the center from which many other emotions emanate, such as anxiety, panic, and depression. Worry levels can range from mild to severe.

THE THREE LEVELS OF WORRY WITH EMOTIONAL RESPONSES

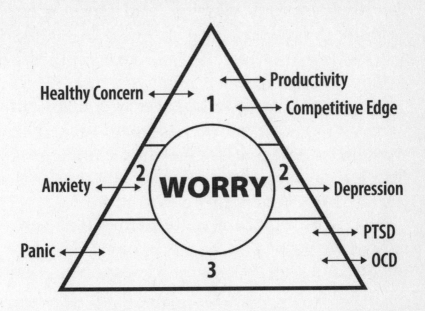

At Level 1, worry is the little voice that alerts you to possible trouble ahead. When you resolve worry at this level, it can provide helpful input regarding the situation that needs to be addressed. It can offer a competitive edge as you consider possible outcomes and develop strategic responses. You can also seek input from your intuitive side or inner spirit to help you to arrive at the best possible solution. At Level 1, you may feel vulnerable but also capable of responding to the challenge.

At Level 2, worry spreads and escalates into the fearful hypervigilance of anxiety or the chronic rumination of depression. You may feel stuck, powerless, and unable to resolve issues and stresses. Your connection to your inner spirit and intuitive guidance erodes. It is easy to feel tense and difficult to feel relaxed and peaceful.

At Level 3, worry erupts into panicky feelings. Worry has now become toxic. Because they may come out of the blue, you cannot find logical reasons for these troubling feelings, which seeds more worry and more anxiety. A loop of fear engages and may spread to more and more situations. Here, exaggeration replaces appropriate analysis and leaves you with the overwhelming feeling that you can't handle the situation. You feel disconnected from your inner spirit and intuitive guidance. Panic attacks, post-traumatic stress disorder (PTSD), and obsessive-compulsive disorder (OCD) are examples of Level 3 worry.

As you can see, the constellation of reactions to worry can vary dramatically. The key to making worry work for you instead of against you is a matter of focus, knowledge, and willingness to change unproductive habits. That is why I wrote this book. My goal is to help you better manage not only your worries but also the stresses that seed your worries. The first step is recognizing both the beneficial and devastating effects of worry. And the good news is that becoming more aware of how your mind is working allows you to begin taking back the reins of control to consciously rewire circuits blown by worry. This time, the wires are strong. This time, they allow positive energy to flow. This time, they directly connect to the highest you, the one who is peaceful and happy.

MY STORY: ANXIETY RESCUE

Before writing *Why Worry?* I published a book in 2007 called *Anxiety Rescue* that not only presented the story of my remarkable recovery from crippling, lifelong anxiety but also shared simple, powerful strategies to stop anxiety dead in its tracks. These experiences with anxiety were also my best teachers. As painful as the lessons felt, I learned what works and what doesn't.

I am a scientist on the faculty of one of the top five medical schools in the country, and a prolific writer with more than 250 articles (often penned under the last name Liszewski) in leading health/science publications. For the past thirty years, I've studied how the immune system works to protect us from infection as well as how it can devastate our bodies when that process goes awry or is overcome by pathogens. In many ways, the biological mechanism of worry is similar to our innate immune system: when held in check, our psychological immune system is designed to help and protect us; allow it to spin out of control, however, and worry — just like an unchecked immune system — can hurt instead of help us.

This is what happened to me. My analytical brain automatically churned out possible scenarios of what could go wrong in any situation, leaving me tense and wary about the unknown future. Like many, I felt that if I worried enough, perhaps it would help me anticipate and thus prevent bad things from happening. Instead, this natural, well-meaning plan became a chronic mental infection.

During my super stressful sophomore year in college, while studying day and night for my finals, I suddenly experienced a sense of overwhelming fear as I reviewed formulas I didn't really understand in my chemistry book. The more I noticed this feeling, the more afraid I became. I wanted to run away, but there was no danger; it just felt like there was. I wondered if I was having a heart attack or losing my mind. I learned later that this experience was a panic or anxiety attack.

I didn't figure that out for quite some time, though, and I continued having episodes, but in more and more situations: driving on the highway, sitting in the classroom, shopping at the grocery store. It seemed that anything could trigger an attack. I was given some sedatives and told by school counselors to relax more. I worried constantly about having these awful feelings. Eventually they subsided, and I was able to bury those troubling emotions. Time helped, but it took several months of confusion and occasional gripping fear. I thought fear was my problem. It didn't occur to me to change my daily stress-producing routine. In other words, I was focusing more on the outcome (fear) than the cause (stress) — on the outside rather than the inside, on the flat tire instead of the nail in the tire. And I learned a great coping mechanism: avoidance. The problem was, how could I avoid waking up in the night and feeling that way? I could always leave class, but I could never leave me.

I spent the next thirty years dealing with anxiety and panic. For a while, I avoided anything that made me feel anxious. I stopped going on vacations, stopped driving on bridges — or just suffered through — and eventually, I stopped leaving my hometown (behavior that continued for more than twenty-five years). Though I went into therapy, tried different medications, and read all the books I could on the subject, I still made only minor progress.

I cried many times and wondered if I would ever overcome my fears, but something inside me never gave up. Something kept searching and hoping.

Maybe that was the helpful aspect of my analytical mind. I'd spent most of my scientific career trying to understand the intricacies of the immune system, asking questions, formulating plans, and then performing experiments to test the hypothesis. If this process didn't give me the answer, I'd start over or revise the experiment for the next time. Even when successful, more experiments were always needed to dig deeper into the subject. As a scientific writer, I was also familiar with taking complex scientific subjects and simplifying them for readers. I had experience in helping to write review articles in prestigious scientific journals and in preparing original journal articles to present new laboratory findings. Could I not use those well-honed skills to help chart a new course for my life as well?

My "Eureka!" moment appeared when I

finally realized that *worry is a choice.* Worry is indeed an inborn response that alerts us to possible trouble, but instead of allowing its dire predictions of future calamities to escalate, I have the power to evaluate it and to react differently. I can choose to hear the voice of worry and disagree; I can choose to maintain harmony with my psychological immune system whose biologic purpose is to help, not hurt.

Here are some other things I learned. Our fears provide valuable lessons. Combining the wisdom and knowledge of our mind, body, and spirit, we can solve any problem. Within each of us is a powerhouse of inner energy that we are seldom aware of; we just have to release it. We can challenge worry and create peace in simple ways. Within us is the power to handle not just some but *all* of our challenges.

NEW HELP FOR ANXIETY AND WORRY
In *Why Worry?* I have added new scientific findings about how the mind works and even more tools and strategies than were included in my earlier book. *Why Worry?* also focuses on the incredible healing power of using holistic strategies that connect our mind, body, and spirit. The message is rather simple: We do not have to be stress-

aholics curled up into a tight ball of worry, fear, and incapacitation. Simply reverse the age-old paradigm of working from the *outside in* (pills, booze, ignoring it) and transform from the *inside out.* Harness the power of focused intention to create positive possibilities instead of imagining catastrophes. Getting over worry — or any problem — is always an "inside job."

One of the first concepts that can supercharge our ability to overcome worry is the recognition of the absolute power held within our thoughts. By first becoming aware of our automatic responses, we harness the secret power of choice. (These tools are described further in chapter 3.)

Although we can choose to make great strides out of the pit of worry, choice alone is not enough. Thundering doubts will persist. This is the protective side of worry. However, we can choose instead to hear a quieter voice that assures us we will be safe and can handle whatever we need to handle. By disagreeing with the doomsday voice, we can amplify another that says, "All is well!"

Now, instead of automatically engaging the worry reflex, we rewire those circuits (described in chapters 4 and 5). Despite the best of intentions, we don't always immediately succeed at everything we try. It takes time to change unproductive lifelong habits. We may stumble along the path and fall back into our old ways. But this too provides a learning opportunity. Here we learn to forgive that which is imperfect. When we release ourselves from the steely grip of perfectionism, our lives become more joyful and less stressful. As we dissolve the need for perfectionism, we allow others to be their imperfect selves. We then learn to flow with the currents of life instead of fighting against the waves. (Those strategies are described in chapter 6.)

One deal breaker that can quickly stall our progress in overcoming worry is failing to recognize and manage our negative mental baggage that is loaded with blame, anger, and guilt. By tackling these emotional barriers, we can help cultivate a mindset for better resolving interactions that cause us pain. We'll also go over new ways to move beyond these limitations and provide the antidotes to blame, anger, and guilt (chapter 7).

Now, here is a question. You are sitting in your new car with a full tank of gas; how far can you go if you don't turn the key to get the car moving? The answer, of course, is nowhere. Thus, overcoming chronic worry is an active, not a passive, process. Our real journey begins when we start to step outside of our comfort zones and take risks to move beyond our limitations and improve our lives.

As you practice challenging yourself in small ways, you will find something miraculous happening. You will begin to feel comfortable and powerful as you face challenges. Risking and doing are far more powerful than worrying and wondering. Not long after I began challenging myself to go farther and farther away from home, I took my first plane flight from Saint Louis to nearby Chicago. There was a thick fog that morning. Although the worry voice was loud, I thanked it for trying to protect me and forged ahead. I boarded the plane with my wonderful friend Pam. I'll never forget the sensation when the plane lifted off the runway. In an instant, the rough and bumpy ride turned silky smooth. We were riding on air and softly ascending into the gentle sky. In between patches of fog, I watched the airport and surrounding houses get smaller.

Then a remarkable thing happened. The fog that blanketed the airplane like swirling smoke just disappeared. In its place was a bright, beautiful, golden sunlight and brilliant blue sky. What an amazing sight for my first airborne view of the heavens. Below us was a pervasive cottony layer of clouds. I beamed and looked over at Pam. She had tears in her eyes. She knew this was a life-altering moment for me. It was a golden flash of victory over a lifelong struggle to release myself from the darkness of my worries and fears. I wasn't crying; my heart was rapidly beating, excited and enthralled. Risk can do that for us. It frees us, it empowers us, and it places us directly back on our life's path. (Tools for learning to expand your comfort zone are described in chapter 8.)

Our journey from worry to peace is incomplete without one more healing aspect: reconnecting to and embracing our inner spirit. This is the doorway to lasting healing. Unfurling and enhancing our connection to our inner spirit can transform the ordinary into the extraordinary. We can access a remarkable realm in which we have the ability to surge beyond self-imposed limitations. We feel happier, more fulfilled, and more guided. One of the signs that this is working is when coincidences begin occurring. (Chapter 9 describes how to embrace your inner spirit and recognize helpful synchronicities.)

Ultimately, it is the combined strength of our mind, body, and spirit that catapults us out of our worries and into peace and power. Combined with knowledge, determination, and flexibility, we can push back the barriers of our limitations. A month after my Chicago flight, I received an invitation to attend an international scientific convention — in Greece! My protective, worrying side immediately fed me dialogues filled with concerns and possible problems. Was I really ready to do this? Could I fly that far, that long, to a foreign country? This could be a catastrophe. What if . . . what if . . . what if . . . But now I could better recognize, hear, and disagree with the loud voice of worry. I countered each negative scenario with something more positive and equally possible. I began to pay attention to the worries that were productive (such as pre-arranging a cab pickup at the airport in Greece, getting local currency to bring, and so on). I disagreed with other worry thoughts and knew that I could use the tools I had developed.

Shortly after booking the flight, I learned that my scientific abstract had been selected for oral presentation. In other words, I would be speaking to a packed audience of international scientists! Again, using every tool I had developed (and a few more), I knew that it was the right time and the right place to go. I knew I had access to help on many levels, and I knew I would accept the invitation. Four months later, I flew to Greece, stood on a podium, looked out over hundreds of world-renowned scientists, cleared my throat, and began my well-rehearsed presentation about how the immune system regulates itself. Here I was, little old me, who trembled at going to the nearby shopping center a few years before, who felt petrified about taking an elevator to the eighteenth floor, who cried in bed late at night because I felt powerless to overcome my fears. After my talk, I reflected on the very surreal moment I had just experienced. I had delivered a message about healing on the physical level while experiencing a deep and profound healing on a personal and spiritual level.

Perhaps that is the most compelling aspect of our journey out of worry: we transform a mindset of lack and limitation into one of fulfillment and power. Although we may not be able to fully comprehend the vast expanses held within the entire meaning of "spirit," we can sense its wonderful presence and the loving strength that connection provides. This places us in a position of power and love, where there is no need for worry.

We all have our demons to face (and that's

plural, not singular). We all have our roads to trek. No one escapes life's challenges, and new tests come with each step. But these difficulties are opportunities to continue growing and expanding. Every time we encounter challenges, we may worry that we cannot forge ahead. We may feel that it's just too hard or too much. But every time we avoid life's challenges, we feel weaker. Only by tackling our challenges can our inner strength grow.

With each new step forward, I wondered, *I did that, but can I really do this?* In answer, I just kept practicing my skills. Each step helped me build on the previous success, but it all began with the *first* decision to go beyond my comfort zone. From there, in spurts forward — with occasional, agonizing setbacks — it was a progression of the spirit. By working on myself, I built on my successes. I forgave myself for my tumbles, and by connecting to my spirit — that boundless source of strength and love — and taking the hand of my frightened inner self, I continue to challenge my limitations. I now know that I can make it over, around, or through any obstacle. Though worry still speaks to me (and I hear it), I thank it for the input it offers and then decide consciously what I will do. I take charge of my own reactions because *worry is a choice.* And there are always options.

You may not have experienced the extremes of worry and fear that I did, but how you react to and handle whatever challenges you face will determine if you are living your life to the fullest or are stalled miserably in struggle. Whatever your specific circumstances are, if you are struggling with worry, this book is for you. I wrote it in a simple style, loaded with practical tips and inspiring stories that I hope will be of help to you. *Why Worry?* is a "from the trenches" approach, providing self-help methods that blend remarkably easy concepts of mind, body, and spirit.

If you feel minimized by your worries, at your wits' end, or hopeless, let me assure you that you can regain control of your life, just as I did. I wrote this book for you. I thought my world was out of control and spinning toward disaster. What I found by working from inside out was a powerhouse of energy I never knew existed. What I found by using these simple ways to challenge worry is that we can create inner peace. What I found by exploring my power within is that we have an internal energy source that never fails. I learned we can handle not just some but all of our worries and stresses. These tools are already available to you. While I cannot guarantee my ideas will work for you, try them, change them to suit your own situation, and go forward step by step. Seek the best possible help on any level. Never, *ever* give up on yourself. Your journey out of worry and into peace and power begins now.

There is a Zen saying that when the student is ready, the teacher appears. I hope that you have come across this book because you are a student of life who has been guided to these powerful, healing words. I also hope you are ready to open yourself up to a journey, not only out of worry, fear, and stress but also directly *into* a life of love, fulfillment, and great peace.

From my spirit to yours,
Kathryn Tristan

1
UNDERSTANDING WHY WE WORRY

Yesterday is history. Tomorrow is a
  mystery.
And today? Today is a gift.
That's why we call it the present.
                    — Babatunde Olatunji

If you are spending more time worrying and less time enjoying life, this book can help you. Worry is a natural part of our biology, designed to serve a useful purpose. We run amok when, instead of allowing it to provide guidance, we focus on dire calamities in the future rather than realistic solutions in the present. Unproductive worrying harms more than it helps.

The goal of this book is to provide you with (a) fresh, new ways of dealing with the stresses that may seed your worries, (b) key strategies for transforming worry into a positive force, and (c) tools to tap into your inner sources of wisdom.

There is a growing body of scientific evidence that helps explain how the brain works and how we can retrain it to overcome unproductive habits. We will explore some of those new, exciting concepts. But we are so much more than our brain and anatomy. The sublime interconnectedness of our mind, body, and spirit provides a powerful way to tune in to inner guidance — once we quiet the thunder of our worry. When you overcome the worry habit, life emerges as a wonderful experience, regardless of your troubles, problems, and challenges. In this space you find greater joy, personal empowerment, and access to a more fulfilling life.

WHY WE WORRY

Life can challenge us in many ways. A natural response is to worry, because the true purpose of worry is to alert us to the need to respond to these challenges. Worry is a dual-edged sword: a positive force that provides a helpful alert or a negative force that overreacts and keeps us stuck. Here are some examples of both. Is your story like one of these?

• Sarah has a presentation to make before her colleagues in a week. She's worried that it isn't good enough. She decides to do more research on the topic and keep polishing it until she is satisfied. Sarah is an example of how to productively worry.

- Chris's son is deployed overseas and most days she worries about his safety. Feeling unsettled was beginning to feel normal. She decided to volunteer at her local USO, welcoming home returning soldiers and assisting their families. Chris shows that while we cannot eliminate worry, we can learn to channel our concerns and focus on something that helps rather than hurts.

- Tim is unemployed and can't find a job. He worries that he'll never find work or be able to pay off his mounting debts. He's miserable, and he sends that energy to everyone around him. Tim isn't using worry to solve his problems; instead, he is creating more problems because of his unproductive reactions.

- Maria is a stay-at-home mother of three. She feels trapped in an unhappy marriage but is afraid to leave. Maria provides an example of how we can fail to seek solutions because we are worried we cannot handle our challenges.

- Doris likes to wonder what could go wrong with anything. She constantly frets, warning her friends and family members to watch out for this and that, and she seldom feels safe doing anything new. Doris is an example of how our personality (high-strung) and learning ("my parents were this way too") can wire our brains into circuits of unproductive behavior.

• Pat cares for an aging mother and aunt, and one of her children has just moved back home. Caught in the middle between the two generations, Pat never seems to have enough time for herself and constantly mulls over her situation. Pat shows us what can happen if we let our worries translate into feelings of helplessness and hopelessness. By giving away her power to her worries, they now run her life.

• Amy, an overworked elementary-school teacher, frequently awakens in the middle of the night with a pounding heart and shortness of breath. She dreads going to bed and is becoming depressed. Her doctor found nothing physically wrong with her and prescribed an antidepressant. Amy provides an example of how stresses can mount from overwork, and how inner worries quickly amplify without conscious awareness.

• Elizabeth's fiancé cheated on her, so she

broke off their engagement. She's says she is now over it, but she recently began to feel anxious when riding elevators and lightheaded while shopping, and now some of these disturbing sensations are coming out of the blue. She was given a clean bill of health but has begun taking sedatives to relax. Elizabeth does not quite realize just how hurt and angry she remains. These powerful buried emotions are severing her connection to her inner sense of safety and are spurting out as anxiety.

What these examples show is that we worry in many different ways and with different levels of intensity. Many of us who suffer from overworry or unhealthy worry are unaware that we are worrying at all, as it has become a normal part of our days, but we may actually feel on edge much of the time. Some cope by using drugs or alcohol, or by keeping super busy. Unfortunately, none of those strategies solve problems. What this book teaches is that managing our worry is an "inside job." Many of us want to work from the outside in, as in some of the coping mechanisms discussed above. But overcoming chronic worry requires us to change from the inside out. What we learn is that we can balance the messages of worry with our reactions to it. We first need to recognize how the rapid-fire response of worry can quickly get out of control.

Snaring those initial, overly worried thoughts can provide the solution to better managing how we worry and what we worry about. It is not so much a matter of *not* having those thoughts, for they are automatic. The key is to become aware of them and consciously respond to them. Our strength to change lies in our ability to choose how we perceive and react, which is empowered by our own conscious intentions.

Here is one of my favorite verses that I've adapted:

Watch your thoughts, for thoughts become words.
Watch your words, for words become attitudes.
Watch your attitudes, for attitudes become actions.
Watch your actions, for actions become habits.
Watch your habits, for habits become character.
Watch your character, for character becomes destiny.

Do you see the pattern? Thoughts → Destiny. Which destiny do you want: worry or authentic power?

HOW WORRY EXPANDS

Those of us battling our worry may find that the more we worry, the more we have to worry about. It keeps coming back or, like a chameleon, changes its color. The automatically expanding nature of worry is something my sister Debbie calls "expandomatic worry." This means that once we begin to worry, the path to a productive outcome can quickly dissolve into doom and gloom. In this way, we unknowingly defeat the purpose of worry or misread a thought of concern and amplify it into a catastrophe. Because so many of our thoughts and reactions are automatic, we may not be aware of how our runaway thoughts even began. The time to evaluate our response to worry is at the very beginning, before the thought mushrooms out of control. Here is an example:

Joan developed a headache in the late afternoon. She focused on that feeling of discomfort and had an immediate thought: What if it's a brain tumor? *Then Joan focused on that and thought,* I'll have to have an MRI. I hate those! I bet I'll feel claustrophobic. *Then Joan wondered,* If it is a brain tumor, will I need chemotherapy or will an operation be best to remove it? *Then Joan considered,* What if it doesn't respond to treatment? Is my will up to date? What will my family do without me? I'll miss my daughter's graduation and never see my grandchildren!

Did you see what happened to Joan within an instant? She rapidly progressed from a simple little headache into a life-threatening disease. It's creative, if not in total error. Instead of evaluating the initial thought, Joan immediately launched into worrying and obsessing over stress-producing scenarios. She could have just taken two aspirin for the headache. An important feature of this type of expanding worry is that, as it grows, it shrinks our sense of safety and comfort. Soon, the watchful, wary eye begins to stay on high alert for anything that might need to be worried about. Just like exercising strengthens our muscles, such re-actions strengthen our habit of worrying. The difference here is that as we strengthen the circuit of hypervigilance, we drain our emotional and physical reserves. It's like running the race, crossing the threshold, and having no energy available for the next race; a mechanism meant to protect has now become harmful.

So what's the problem? After all, lots of people have concerns. The difference is in how you let them affect your life. Worry becomes a problem when it escalates to the point where it robs your life of joy, and when you begin to focus on your worries instead of living life to the fullest. When this happens, worry controls you. You begin to live in a more anxious state, waiting for the next bad thing to happen. When you expect a negative outcome, it can become a self-fulfilling destiny. Thus, by agreeing with worry, you give it power that prompts you to watch out for anything that could be similarly worrisome. By agreeing with worry, you expand it. By agreeing with worry, you're launched into the troubling world of anxiety.

When we experience anxiety, we have supersized our worries. Anxiety not only results from worrying but can also seed further worrying. Not everyone responds in this way, however. Are we programmed to do so? For some of us, why does anxiety so often override our ability to think clearly and productively?[1] New research demonstrates that our irrational emotions can utterly overrule our more temperate rational minds. The brain is hardwired to respond this way. The old paradigm was that the body reacted based on a rapid and coordinated analysis of the situation, but scientific evidence provided by researcher Joseph LeDoux, PhD, at New York University, found that we respond emotionally *before* we respond cerebrally.[2] Thus, irrationality trumps rationality with breathtaking efficiency as sensory signals (what we see, hear, feel, smell, and taste) are translated into thoughts and rapid responses.

In the blink of an eye, our brains initiate a cascade of reactions that flood the body with biochemicals of alarm and action. While our first reaction is hardwired, we can retain, elongate, or retract subsequent responses. Thus, following the quick burst of energy, our conscious minds begin to evaluate what to do next. It is in this second response that our power lies.

Worry establishes itself as a problem when we do not use this second response to turn off the automatic reaction. Worry then elongates our natural reactions, fires them with imaginative negative outcomes, fuels them with fearful anticipation, and exaggerates what could happen. Now worry amplifies into anxiety.

The problem is that worry and anxiety are red flags. They are supposed to alert us to the possibility of trouble, danger, and harm. These warnings worked wonderfully millions of years ago, when we had to worry about where our next meal was coming from, whether or not we were safe from saber-toothed tigers, and how we were to propagate the species.

In our modern world, overstimulation can quickly erode an evolutionary mechanism that was meant to be helpful, not harmful. Over a period of time, our negative reactions develop into quick-firing neural circuits that become wired in our brains and bodies. Our minds and bodies become accustomed to following the negative training we are providing: the training to overreact, overstress, and overworry. The myriad interactions in which we participate every day — our jobs, finances, relationships, and so on — can drain our energy resources, leaving us on an autopilot that idles in a constant state of feeling overwhelmed and anxious.

When worry becomes supersized into anxiety, it is sending us a message. The angst we feel comes from the impossible demand to control the outside world. However, true control lies within. True control

37

releases us from the need for total control. True control is strengthened by our conscious intention to work from inside out and in connection with our mind, body, and spirit.

TAPPING INTO YOUR CORE POWER

There are four key strategies or steps for managing chronic worry and fear. You are meant to have a wonderful life. It is within your reach. All you need to master is a simple set of tools that help you find the power that's already within you; this incredible power lies *within,* not without. Most of us never quite know how to access and manifest all that we want. Our worries and fears hold us back.

You can move beyond worry by reconnecting to your inner core of safety and power using these four key concepts. I call these CORE concepts because they draw on your *inner* resources, pull them back to the surface, and become your foundation for restoring balance in your life. Each concept provides practical ways to change. You begin by quickly and easily drawing a road map for your own recovery. Each step forward is a step away from worry. Each tiny change amplifies the next. By your own design, you take back your life and create one of purpose, power, and enjoyment.

Each CORE concept builds on the previous one. Each step empowers the next. At the very core of your worry lies the troubling perception that you are powerless. But you are the only one who *does* have the power, believe it or not. Power comes from the choices you make. If you don't recognize your power of choice, you may feel swept along by the quick currents of life. Whether you realize it or not, you *do* have control over how you choose to view any problem or challenge. You can change the immediate, hardwired response, the exaggerated mental meanderings, and your subsequent overreactions. For example, instead of responding with anger to the behavior of others, you can learn to step back, observe, and then choose how you will respond. Choice provides unmitigated strength and unfailing power. In our dealings with others, situations, or challenges, a peaceful and directed mind finds many solutions. The choices we make are entirely up to us. It takes time to permanently overcome worry; you didn't get this way overnight, and you won't conquer it overnight, either. But by rebuilding a more solid foundation, you *can* quickly begin to feel better and more in charge of your life again. It takes time to change habits and patterns. But it's worth your time and effort.

This is not a passive process. You are the driver, not the passenger, in the journey out of worry. You can read all the books on the subject, attend lectures, roam from therapist to therapist, and take a variety of medications, but to transform permanently, you must rescue yourself and take charge of your own healing.

These four CORE concepts help you change how you view your life. They will provide a template for experiencing the magic and joy of life. And they will help you learn how to empower yourself and stop worry from being your driver. Each concept builds on the previous one, and you progress at your own pace. Here's a quick summary of these tools.

The *C* in CORE stands for *Choice.* Healing from fear begins by recognizing that your life is built on your choices. This initial concept reveals a secret: choice provides power. How you react to any situation, event, or experience is something you choose. You overcome chronic worrying when you begin making power-building, rather than fear-seeding, choices.

The *O* stands for *Outlook.* This second concept reveals that how you think about anything determines how you experience everything. By changing how you perceive, process, and react to any situation, you surge past seemingly insurmountable problems. You can create safety and feel more powerful. You can deconstruct inner trash talk and negative thinking, and consciously rewire, retrain, and restore more productive ways of reacting to worries and challenges. Ultimately, you launch into your own recovery by taking charge of two natural inner forces that either hurt or heal. Changing your outlook is a key strategy to overcoming worry.

R stands for learning to take *Risks.* Worriers don't embrace the idea of doing anything risky, anything that might heighten an already overactive sense of danger. But embracing your ability to make better choices and connect with inner sources of strength reenergizes your self-confidence and allows you to take small steps away from worry. As confidence builds, you begin to free yourself from the prison of chronic worry. You learn how to tone down the voice that says "don't" and amplify the one that says "do!" You learn how to reenergize feelings of happiness and realize that taking risks may not be so risky. Instead, you find you are your own source of safety in any situation. You find that risks can lead to fun, exploration, and adventure. You find that worry fades like a bad memory, while excitement for life emerges.

E stands for *Embracing Spirit.* When you embrace your inner spirit, you cultivate the highest part of yourself that loves life, gives direction through your feelings, and perceives meaning beyond the five senses. As you continue pushing back the barriers that have hindered you, "overwhelmed" and "defeated" are no longer in your personal vocabulary. Embracing your inner spirit and your intuitive side allows you to surge beyond limitations and head into the remarkable. It releases a buried treasure. It rejuvenates a childlike sense of wonder, imagination, and adventure. This treasure is expansive and fun. When you feel free and safe enough to explore instead of recoil, you do things you never thought you could, and by turning your pain into an opportunity for growth and healing, you open the door to becoming the person you've always wanted to be.

This book may not have all the answers, but there are some exciting and helpful ideas — ideas that are from personal experience and from others who've taken this journey. Take what works for you, develop your own modifications, and continue to seek the best help available.

If you want to change, you can. If you want to heal, you will. If you want to take back the reins of control, you just begin. You've suffered long enough. Now is the time to try something new, something better, something fun. Are you ready?

Notes

1. Jerilyn Ross and Robin Cantor-Cooke, *One Less Thing to Worry About: Uncommon Wisdom for Coping with Common Anxieties* (New York: Ballantine Books, 2009). This question was posed by former president and CEO of the Anxiety and Depression Association of America, the late Jerilyn Ross, who struggled with anxiety and panic earlier in her life. She later became an internationally recognized psychotherapist and one of the nation's leading experts on anxiety disorders. Jerilyn related her own experience that occurred while she was working out in a gym. She repetitively lifted 130 pounds on an assisted pull-up exercise machine. Just as she raised the weights during one lift, her nearby cell phone rang. Instantly, she jumped up to answer it while the weights came crashing

down, almost causing a serious injury to her nearby trainer. "Why did I do this?" she later wondered. There was no emergency. Her reactions represented a seemingly automatic response without the benefit of conscious thought to temper them. This inspired Jerilyn to look into scientific studies to see if they could provide some answers.

2. Joseph LeDoux, *Synaptic Self: How Our Brains Become Who We Are* (New York: Viking, 2002).

2
THE WORRY SPECTRUM

I have been through some terrible
things in my life, some of which
actually happened.
— Mark Twain

It's time to examine *how* we worry and how
our automatic stress-producing mindset
keeps us dangling on the high wires of tension. But worry is not all bad; it can also
protect and help us to worry smart. When
we worry smart, we calmly assess situations,
steer a path through the challenge, or move
into greater achievement. Knowing the difference is what will determine whether our
worries arm us or harm us.

Those of us who fret are great thinkers.
We love to analyze, dramatize, and dissect
our lives. We also have perfected a little
character trait called *worry* that keeps us
hyperalert and ready to respond to anything
we consider threatening. We know worry

inside and out. It is a part of our makeup; it is what seems normal. But worry is a dual-edged sword that can harm as much as it can protect.

The word *worry* is ancient and found in many languages: The Anglo-Saxon *wyrgan* or German *würgen* are translated as to strangle or injure; Middle English variants *wirwen* and *worien* mean choke; and the Indo-European *wergh* means wormlike. So our ancestors knew about worry. They knew that once it worms its way into your life, it can become a harmful habit.

I know firsthand that this is true. And I'm not the only one. One day, as I was waiting in line at a pharmacy, I noticed on the counter a little cross-stitched plaque that read: "I'm so used to being nervous that, when I'm not nervous, it makes me nervous!"

Isn't that also true of worry? Unfortunately, constant worry fuels anxiety and creates a chronically unsettled mindset. If you anticipate that something bad is going to happen, it makes sense that you feel nervous. But over time, your body locks into a biochemical mode that responds to your unconscious directions. Worry and nervousness become personality traits, your natural idle. That makes it difficult to know *what* bothers you because *everything* does.

New scientific findings are helping to shed light on how this happens. One of the most exciting breakthroughs in neuroscience is the discovery that our thoughts and feelings can change the very fabric and function of our brains. This young science, called neuroplasticity, describes the astonishing process of how the brain can wire and rewire itself. *Neuro* refers to nerve cells (neurons) and *plastic* suggests malleability or changeability.

Norman Doidge, MD, describes this new science and its revolutionary implications in his book *The Brain that Changes Itself.*[1] He also provides case studies showing how lives have been changed — emotional and learning disorders healed, stroke patients cured, and even aging brains renewed.

Our brains have approximately 100 billion neurons, which can fire electrical impulses often lasting less than one thousandth of a second. Further, each neuron can connect electrochemically with up to ten thousand other neurons. This complex network creates an amazing web that governs our movements, feelings, and thoughts. Scientists are still trying to define exactly what this web is, but one thing is clear: our brains are amazingly adaptable.

Some scientific experiments have even shown how brain anatomy can be shaped by thoughts and intentions alone. Alvaro Pascual-Leone, PhD, MD, utilized a technology called transcranial magnetic stimulation (TMS)[2] to create a brain map of an area called the motor cortex. Dr. Pascual-Leone taught two groups (who had never studied piano) a sequence of keyboard notes. One group practiced on a piano keyboard two hours a day for five days, while the other group only imagined they were playing (and hearing the sound). At the end of the five-day period, the mental practice group had created the same physical brain map as the group who actually played the music. Thus, action as well as imagination can activate the same parts of the brain. What we think about can have physical implications and consequences.

Richard J. Davidson, PhD, and Sharon Begley extend the ideas of neuroplasticity into the realm of transforming our "emotional styles."[3] Just as we all have unique fingerprints, we also possess a constellation of responses and reactions that constitute our own inimitable emotional profile. One key element of this profile is resilience, i.e., how we bounce back from our problems. It turns out that people who score high on this attribute show a brain map of increased activity in the left side of the prefrontal cortex. This area has large bundles of neurons that are spliced into the brain's alarm center and may send calming signals to the region. In this way, our thinking brain can calm our emotional brain. Thus, practices such as mindfulness meditation can be effective means of rewiring our nerve circuitry, in particular by increasing neural connections designed for calming rather than alerting.

Of course, we all worry sometimes. When it genuinely helps to solve problems or alert us to real danger, worry can be a powerful means for protection and productivity. Our goal is not to eliminate all worry but to learn how to respond to it in a way that helps, not harms. For example, worry can be the twinge of thought that suggests you see the doctor when something is wrong — an appointment that might reveal a potential health problem just in time. Worry can also be the internal prodding that suggests you take a cab instead of walking home at night — a decision that may save you from being mugged.

Concern about how well you will do for an upcoming presentation may help you polish it to a higher level of professionalism.

Concern about the competition in business may help steer you on a more productive and successful path. Concern about health may help you eat better and exercise. In these cases, worry has the positive effect of helping you deal constructively with intimidating or challenging situations. Whether it's business, competitive sports, or just living, knowing how to worry smart allows you to improve your life.

It makes sense to embrace the positive aspects of worry. This biological balancing act is a well-honed response developed over millions of years. We are the descendants of an unbroken line of survivors who were smarter, reacted faster, and worried enough to stay safe. Worrying is a hardwired defense mechanism that can help us think, plan, and organize our responses to avoid perceived threats. Also hardwired is our fight-or-flight response for when worrying doesn't help us avoid the problem. The powerful fight-or-flight reaction provokes a lightning-like, energy-bolstering response. Thus, worrying is a slow burn designed to help us avoid fighting or fleeing. It was designed to help.

Worry coordinates the reactions of millions of the body's cells. Physiologically, the body's alarm circuit lies deep within the brain in the small, almond-shaped amygdala. This small organ is critical for decoding emotions, especially when they are perceived as alerting us to a threat. Some scientists suggest that fear is the response to physical danger, while its cousin anxiety is the psychological response to perceived danger. Imagine that you are walking home at night down a dark street. No one is around. You begin to feel apprehensive and nervous. You quicken your pace and can't wait to get home. These sensations come from the *possibility* that someone might attack you, although there is nothing that is specifically threatening you. Rather, it is your interpretation of the *possibility* that something bad could happen that causes you to feel anxious.

On the other hand, fear is a response to a definite threat. If someone jumps out at you, points a gun, and demands your wallet, the danger becomes real, not imaginary. Other research by Dr. Joseph LeDoux, found that the brain catalyzes a bodily response to sensory input before it analyzes the input. That means our automatic responses occur *before* our cerebral (rational) responses.[4]

Although fear and anxiety have different focuses, they share common reactions and feelings. The anxiety causes fear, while the fear can also result in anxiety. The constellation of reactions can be similar because what we imagine can be just as powerful as what is real.

New brain mapping studies have located fear and anxiety in different but interacting regions of the amygdala. Persistent anxiety can be traced to the chronic idling of the fear response in a circuitry called the hypothalamic-pituitary-adrenal axis (or HPA axis). The engine that keeps the fear idling may be fueled by another brain region called the bed nucleus of the stria terminalis (BNST). The BNST is activated by adrenaline that spurts out of our adrenal glands after the fear response engages.

The adrenals also pump out approximately thirty other hormones, and chief among them is cortisol, which is often called the "stress hormone" because it can be found in higher concentrations in anxious and stressed individuals. While cortisol's initial effects are swift and dramatic, its long-term presence is bad for your biology because it hampers your immune system and leads to a host of other conditions. It was meant to create a brief, powerful, and limited response.

A chronic worrier is an individual who is on edge and prepared for dangers that do not happen. He or she is constantly poised for danger, ready to react. For example, a woman at the sink cleaning up dishes after a long, stressful day may become suddenly startled by the presence of a looming figure that unexpectedly approaches out of the blue and touches her. Heart racing, breath quickening, a sense of electricity coursing through her body, she quickly turns around to discover her husband, who just came into the kitchen. In a chronic worrier, the startle reaction may occur more frequently and in a host of situations.

So, are we at the mercy of our brains? If we have programmed ourselves, by our biology and learning, are we stuck with that response? There's good news: the answer is no. There are a number of sciences that are beginning to unravel the complexities of how we can change our programming and rewire some of those biological circuits.

One of the fastest evolving and most exciting fields in science is called epigenetics. *Genetics* refers to genes, your DNA blueprints; *epi* means *in addition to* or *around* genes. Epigenetics studies how genes are turned off or on. A gene's environment is critical, contributing to whether it is active or inactive, as chemical groups bind and modify how genes are expressed into protein. Further, once changes occur to turn a gene off or on, these changes can be inherited.

According to Bruce Lipton, PhD, a pioneer in the field of science and spirit, our genes are influenced by our beliefs as well as our physical environment.[5] Lipton's studies suggest that the information provided by environmental signals controls our biology on a single-cell level — as well as affecting multicellular organisms like humans. Our responses to this environmental information are influenced by our perceptions, but perceptions can be true or false. This means: *Beliefs control biology.* Perceptions are our beliefs. Perceptions are the keys to the kingdom.

What might all this mean for worriers? We are not stuck with our genes or self-defeating behaviors. How we think or choose to think can influence our negative traits by changing our inner biochemistry. Our thoughts can also alter our physical state. The ability to change our thoughts has powerful ramifications for restructuring and improving our lives.

Take the example of the placebo effect, the phenomenon in which some people's health improves by taking a pill that does not contain the medicine. According to Dr. Lipton, though it is often dismissed as quackery, the placebo effect stands as a testament to the amazing power of the mind to heal the body. No one quite knows how it works, but a placebo can change the biochemistry of our reactions just as a medication does. In one study, 80 percent of the effect of antidepressant medications, as assessed in clinical trials, could be attributed to the placebo effect.[6] Further, the placebo effect can translate into measurable physical healing. Thus, the message is that learning how to harness your mind can make the difference between living a life of fear, worry, and illness or one of peace and health.

Knowing the incredible power of our thoughts to direct our lives, for better or for worse, provides a strong impetus to more carefully evaluate, consider, and test our beliefs. Knowledge is power! Tuning in to and understanding how our minds work and speak to us is a key first step.

THE TRIGGER FINGER OF FEAR

The above science describes some of the emerging knowledge of the amazing impact of our thoughts on our well-being as well as on our dysfunction. But there is so much more to this than how our brains function. Our worries impact our mind, body, and spirit. Worry can cause us to feel tense and unsettled when we stew but don't solve the problem. Our inner connections to feelings of safety become frayed. We begin to set up a circuit of worry-stress-worry: when our worries are not productively addressed, they may actually amplify our concerns, leading to more stress, and feeling more stressed may make us more worried. At the heart of the problem lie our thoughts and fearful assumptions. When we constantly worry, we are living life on the edge and can easily overreact because of the incessant negative chatter of our mind. Our triggers are many, and our finger is ready to pull.

For me, worry took the form of frequently feeling on edge without knowing why. At other times, I could pinpoint that I was feeling nervous, but didn't know what to do about it. I didn't recognize that I was worrying constantly. Ignoring my unsettled feelings got to be a habit — another talent of worriers is the robotlike ability to suppress feelings if we don't understand or want to deal with them.

Our thoughts can be all over the place.

I'm unhappy
This isn't right
I'm really mad

I should be . . . no, I shouldn't . . . or
   should I?
I can't do anything about this
Things will never be any better
WHAT IF . . .
What if . . .
What if . . .

How often does worry percolate into your personality? Can you distinguish types of nervousness? For several years, I coached my daughter's elementary school basketball team. This was like the blind leading the blind. I was a good basketball player in my youth, but I hadn't a clue as to how to coach a team. I spent my lunches huddled over library books about coaching girls' basketball (most of which were quite dated — apparently it's not a hot topic). Before the games, I often felt anxious. I could identify the feeling of being nervous about a specific event, and I really wasn't upset by *that* feeling. But many other times, I just didn't feel right and could not figure out the cause.

To better manage our worries, then, it is important that we understand how we are worrying and to distinguish different types of worry; otherwise, worry can worm its way into our life automatically. You may have been unconsciously practicing this trait for years. Can you trace it back to when you were younger? I can.

In my junior year of high school, I changed schools. We couldn't afford the private high school I had attended the first two years, so I transferred to a public school. There were a lot of changes. We didn't wear uniforms, so I needed a wardrobe. That meant needing to decide what to wear each day, and of course, it had to be cool — certainly not plaid skirts, white blouses, and plain shoes. The school, the classmates, and the teachers were all new to me. Initially, I felt like an outsider who didn't fit in. Worry started worming its way into my daily thinking habits, as I wondered who I would sit with at lunch, who I would talk to between classes, or even just who might think that what I was wearing was unfashionable.

At about the same time, my family took a trip to a state park, where we went on a tour of a large, well-known cave. As we got into the middle of the cave, the guide abruptly turned off the lights to show us how truly dark it was. I had never liked the dark as a child, and the plunge into total darkness unnerved me. A lightning bolt of fear hit. I didn't say anything or react outwardly, but I found my mother's hand and held it until the guide turned the lights back on. For the remainder of the cave hike, I worried that the lights would go off again.

Shortly after that, I started feeling uncomfortable riding in the backseats of cars or any place I couldn't quickly leave. The pangs of apprehension had been amplifying and the expanding nature of fear had begun to kick in and chisel away at my life.

What I didn't realize then was that anxiety can boil over from worry just like heating a pot of water. In this case stress fuels the fires. The time to intercede is *before* it makes a mess. The time to act is *before* it goes out of control. The time to make changes is before worry gets to the point of boiling over into anxiety. You do this by learning to recognize the warning signs of intensifying stress. For chronic worriers, that can be a challenge.

THE WORRY SPECTRUM

Learning to identify when you automatically kick into the worry mode is a key-first challenge. Only when you become aware of your mental chatter can you consciously choose to transform your harmful reactions into productive responses. Worry is energy. It is just like sunlight that passes through a prism to create a rainbow of colors. In this case, the light is your experience, the prism is your mind, and the colors are your thoughts.

More than three hundred years ago, Sir Isaac Newton found that when he passed white light through a triangular piece of glass, it spread out into its component colors, the spectrum of light. Further, when he put the light back through a second prism, it became white once again. Rainbows occur when the sun shines onto the collective prisms of water droplets in the air, dispersing the light waves into their component spectrum: red, orange, yellow, green, blue, indigo, and violet.

When we worry, it's as if light waves are coming through our consciousness. They can disperse in many ways. The key here is that we can choose our own colors, our own reactions. When we do not choose consciously, worry filters through our experiences and unconsciously emerges as our old, automatic, and unproductive way of reacting. The choice is ours.

This is how the worry spectrum works.

What is the color of your worry?

RED: When your worry waves are red, you are tense, uptight, and scared much of the time. Because of this, your body and mind can kick into worry quickly. You may experience generalized anxiety — that is, you are afraid of many things, including the feeling of fear itself. Perhaps you've had anxiety or panic attacks at some point and now worry about them returning. You may have even visited the emergency room for chest pain or dizziness, only to be told you are fine. Red worry can be resolved by realizing how your life stresses overwhelm you, and then taking steps to recognize and understand your feelings in order to regain your balance.

ORANGE: When your worry waves are orange, you feel disconnected from life and constantly stressed. You only see the problems in your life and you focus intently on them. It's hard to relax and harder still to find solutions to all that vexes and disturbs you, because you are fixated on what is wrong. Orange worry can be resolved by recognizing your ability to creatively seek alternative, positive solutions.

YELLOW: When your worry waves are yellow, you feel powerless in resolving your worries. This is the land of depression, a dark and sad place. When you feel powerless and vulnerable, it is hard to solve any of the problems that worry you. Now you are also worried about yourself, but feel things can't get better. Yellow worry can be resolved by decreasing your sense of vulnerability and building feelings of self-empowerment.

GREEN: When your worry waves are green, you may be feeling a great deal of heartache. Perhaps you've lost someone close to you, had an important relationship end, or lost a job that you loved. This level can also feel sad, especially because you constantly focus on what went wrong, what should have happened, or what could have been. Accepting the reality of the situation is difficult because, in your mind, you keep trying to change it. Perhaps you don't feel trustful of the world or confident enough to begin another relationship or seek that dream job. Green worry can be resolved by enhancing self-nurturing and self-love.

BLUE: When your worry waves are blue,

you may feel held back and can't quite easily express yourself. Instead of speaking your mind, you clam up. Instead of becoming the artist you dreamed about, you go daily to your accounting job. Instead of fulfilling your desires, you keep them inside. You do all this and yet you worry that you don't feel happy in your daily life. Blue worry can be resolved by learning how to better recognize, evaluate, and communicate your feelings.

INDIGO: When your worry waves are the blue-purple color of indigo, you have begun to figure out and understand worry. You recognize that it can provide a way to get an upper edge on life, relationships, jobs, and so on. At this level, you begin to embark on a journey of knowing. You become open to new experiences and trustful of your destiny. At this level, you begin to better hear the voice of intuition and its deep connection to knowing. You are awake to possible troubles and can better steer clear of them.

VIOLET: When you have reached the level of violet, your worries are few and your connections to your spiritual side of life are many. You automatically and easily connect to your life and whatever challenges it brings. You recognize life for the journey it is and value all of your experiences. You let go of control and let your life unfold as it needs to, regardless of your circumstances.

Just like an artist's palette, the colors of worry can be blended. By recognizing how these colors play out in your life, you arm yourself with an arsenal of knowledge and power. You have a choice. You get to choose how worry filters through your mind. Do you want to live your life directed by your worries, fears, and need for control? If not, then it is time to take charge of how you worry.

HOW TO WORRY SMART

Here's a news flash:

Although you can't necessarily change life, you can change how you *react* to it!

You can stop worry dead in its tracks by remembering this deceptively simple concept. That is, once you recognize you are in an overworry mode, you can consciously make different choices.

Your true power lies within, not without.

The Worrywart Quiz™

Score yourself on each question of this self-assessment quiz.

	Often	Sometimes	Rarely
Do you feel edgy and on guard?	◯	◯	◯
Do you overreact?	◯	◯	◯
Do you assume the worst will happen?	◯	◯	◯
If you make a mistake, does it bother you a lot?	◯	◯	◯
Are you upset when things don't go perfectly?	◯	◯	◯
Do you have trouble falling asleep?	◯	◯	◯
Do you start worrying as soon as you awaken?	◯	◯	◯
Do you feel that worrying shows you care?	◯	◯	◯
Do you think something bad might happen if you do not worry?	◯	◯	◯
Are you worried that you are worried?	◯	◯	◯

Score 3 for Often, 2 for Sometimes, and 1 for Rarely.

    Low-Level Worrier 10–14

    Moderate Worrier 15–20

    High Worrier 21–30

Note: This quiz is not for a professional assessment.

It comes from your ability to choose. Cultivating this mindset allows you to connect with internal sources of wisdom and guidance. Paradoxically, by giving up the need to control the outside world, you empower yourself with a greater command of your life.

You can take a quantum leap toward overcoming worry by making a fundamental shift into a different mindset. As you shift your perceptions, you transform your reality. By understanding *how* your thoughts and worries constrict your life, you open the portal to create positive changes. Toss out worry and instead load up on knowledge and understanding. These supplies are light, yet immensely powerful for helping you walk out of the pit of worry.

You have already taken your first steps by reading this book. You have seen and better understand how you worry in unhealthy ways. Equipped with this knowledge and a bit of soul searching, you have the power to engage a greater command of your life. Now, the negative effects of worry will dissolve more easily as you more quickly and productively change your thought patterns and reactions. Knowing where you are on the worry spectrum is important if you are to better understand not only how you worry but also how to deal with your worries.

Chapter Summary

- Worry is a natural mechanism designed to help us solve problems.
- Constant nonproductive worrying creates a stress-filled mindset.
- Worry can make you feel edgy, on guard, and crabby, and can interfere with sleep.
- We differ in how we react to stress. We learn as well as inherit behavioral tendencies that translate stresses more easily into worry, anxiety, and depression.
- Neither your past actions nor your biology chain you to worry. You can take a quantum leap out of fear and into healing as soon as you start making better choices about how you think about your challenges.
- When we worry, it is like light waves coming through our consciousness. It can disperse in a spectrum of colors or types.
- Our power to use worry productively is a matter of conscious choice.
- Although you can't necessarily change what happens, you can choose how to react to it!

Notes

1. Norman Doidge, *The Brain That Changes Itself: Stories of Personal Triumph from the Frontiers of Brain Science* (New York: Penguin Books, 2007). Dr. Doidge describes the new science of neuroplasticity and its revolutionary implications. He also provides case studies showing how lives have been changed: emotional and learning disorders healed, stroke patients cured, and even aging brains renewed.
2. Ibid.
3. Richard J. Davidson and Sharon Begley, *The Emotional Life of Your Brain: How Its Unique Patterns Affect the Way You Think, Feel, and Live — and How You Can Change Them* (New York: Hudson Street Press, 2012). In their book, the authors extend the ideas of neuroplasticity into the realm of transforming our "emotional styles."
4. Joseph LeDoux, *Synaptic Self: How Our Brains Become Who We Are* (New York: Viking, 2002).
5. Bruce H. Lipton, *The Biology of Belief: Unleashing the Power of Consciousness, Matter & Miracles* (New York: Hay House, 2008). Dr. Lipton performed scientific studies that placed identical stem cells into three different types of solutions for

growth. Depending on the nutrients in which they grew, cells formed into three distinctly different types of cells (bone, muscle, and fat), despite having the exact same genetic blueprint. Thus, the environment of the cell may directly affect how the cells respond.

6. Irving Kirsch, Thomas J. Moore, Alan Scoboria, and Sarah S. Nicholls, "The Emperor's New Drugs: An Analysis of Antidepressant Medication Data Submitted to the U.S. Food and Drug Administration," *Prevention & Treatment* 5, no. 23 (American Psychological Association, 2002).

■ ■ ■ ■

CORE CONCEPT 1:
I ALWAYS HAVE
CHOICES

■ ■ ■ ■

3
WAKING UP TO YOUR HIDDEN POWERS:
AWARENESS AND CHOICE

The ancestor to every action in the physical world is a thought.
— Ralph Waldo Emerson

To begin taking back the reins of control, you first must wake up. It may not seem like you are slumbering when worry and fear dominate your life, but both numb your sense of joy and adventure. You are constantly vigilant about the possible dangers of a situation, rather than experiencing the excitement and pleasure it may hold. You become distrustful of life and wish to control the world so that you and everyone you care about are safe and sound. On the surface, this makes sense. But it is the balance of logical concerns and chronic worry that determines whether you are enjoying your life or merely coping with it. A worried mind sees fewer possibilities; it primarily focuses on what is wrong about a situation instead of what is right. An expansive mind sees a positive outcome and perceives potential.

Your recovery from worry and fear begins when you learn to become aware of the internal powerhouse that only you possess — the power of choice. Overcoming worry is less about eliminating it than it is about recognizing how to productively deal with the stresses and struggles that seed it. Becoming peaceful despite your challenges means learning to make better *choices* in how you view and deal with them.

CORE concept 1 states:

I always have choices.

What does this mean? Did you *choose* to lose your job? Did you *choose* that the truck would hit your car and leave you injured? Did you *choose* to get stuck in this snowstorm?

Of course not. Let's face it: We exert very little control over the external events of our lives. But control and choice differ dramatically. Control is the attempt to command and dictate what happens externally in your life, while choice directs what happens internally. Choice provides the only true control you'll ever possess. That is the seat of your power. Thus, your control lies within and comes from your ability to exercise the power of choice.

I Always Have Choices means:

> You can't necessarily control what happens to you, but you can control your reaction. You *choose* how to react.

This shift in thinking allows you to replace false power (which eventually fails) with authentic power (which always succeeds). False power relies upon external forces that are not subject to your control. Authentic power is something that you own, that is yours, that no one can take away from you. It arises from your ability to choose how you react to any challenge. All else can be taken from you, except your authentic power, the power to direct and command your own thoughts. As a result, true control lies in releasing the need to control your outside world and instead taking charge of your inside world.

How can you access this authentic power? Try the following exercise:

> Point to yourself.

Don't think about it; just point to yourself.

75

Now look where you are pointing. Are you pointing to your head? Are you pointing to your toes?

Most people point to their heart, not their head or other places. What does that mean? It suggests that who we truly are lies less in our ever-analyzing brain and more in our emotional core — the feeling part of us that is represented by our heart.

In our heart, we identify with our higher feelings. Our heart symbolizes abstract concepts such as intuition, soul, and of course, love. Our heart also mediates strong feelings such as sadness and fear; the energy of a rapidly beating heart can come from both the excitement of joy and the pangs of apprehension.

When we experience heartfelt love for ourselves, for another, or even for an activity we are engaged in, we are at peace, happy, and in a place that feels good and right. But when we feel bad, our chest can literally ache. You may have seen things that are "heartbreaking," or have experienced a "heavy heart" or "heartache," and you may have heard it said that so-and-so "didn't have the heart to do it."

The importance of the heart as an emotional center has been recognized since ancient times. The Greek philosopher Aristotle taught that the heart is the center of thought, emotion, and intelligence. The Egyptians felt that the heart was the seat of the soul as well as of thought, emotion, and memory. After death, according to dictates in the Egyptian *Book of the Dead*, the deceased's heart would be weighed. Leading a virtuous life kept the heart light, while leading a less virtuous life caused the heart to enlarge. Only "lighthearted" people were allowed into the afterlife. Indeed, even today many metaphysical teachers suggest that the heart-mind connection is a powerful and dynamic circuit and a gateway into the realm of mind-body-spirit.

REWIRING WORRY: EARL VERSUS PEARL

Regardless of how we interpret the importance of the heart, it is clear that when you are worried and afraid, many things are happening in your body, but your pounding heart is the nucleus of this reaction. To repair and rewire the worry circuit, you need to work from the inside out and start, symbolically, at the level of your heart. That is, you gain access to your CORE power by becoming more aware of your thoughts and feelings. Focusing your attention on the mind-heart connection allows you to do that.

Before we begin this process, let's talk about two opposing aspects of your heart center. These are polarities with different functions. One focuses on protection while the other focuses on peacefulness. I have given these aspects names to reflect the constellations of feelings and reactions they represent.

The first one is EARL.

Exaggerating
Angry
Rigid
Limiting

EARL is never satisfied with anything and constantly chatters about concerns and worries. EARL exaggerates and easily feels anger and anxiety. EARL trusts no one and offers worrisome thoughts of caution, wariness, and withdrawal in order to keep you safe from that which is unknown or threatening. This aspect remembers all the things that have ever frightened you and doesn't want them to recur. It wants to hold you back from moving too far out there, to keep you safe from harm. EARL energy is like your own police department, whose motto is "To Serve and Protect."

EARL is that inner force that tries to stop you from encountering possible dangers. EARL is not bad; its desire is to protect. EARL wants you to worry and be fearful as a means of keeping you and others safe and sound.

If worry has a grip on your life, you know EARL very well.

But there's another aspect of your heart zone — PEARL. PEARL is much more relaxed and fun. PEARL is fearless and believes that everything will work out just fine. PEARL feels confident that you can handle anything that comes along. This aspect gives selflessly, laughs frequently, and loves to play. It is the whisper of joy and contentment when you feel love for someone or something.

Peaceful
Earnest
Adventurous
Resilient
Loving

Each of us has an EARL side and a PEARL side. Simply put, we have two competing sides of our spirit; we can be peaceful, joyful, positive, and loving but also worried, fearful, anxious, and angry. Some call these sides "higher self" and "lower self." While the word *high* often represents positive and *low* negative, there is actually no good or bad, right or wrong, in this instance. There are just two polarities, like in a magnet. There is one that attracts and one that repels. There is one that is up and one that is down. Both of these polarities can be of help, but balance is the key. For example, we need to be careful, but when we are too careful, we may not take the risks we need to follow our dreams. We need to be fearless, except if there is danger present.

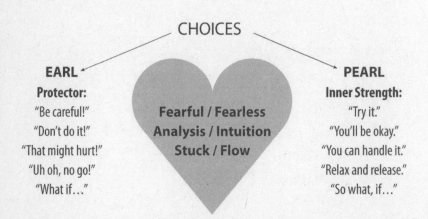

CHOICES

EARL
Protector:
"Be careful!"
"Don't do it!"
"That might hurt!"
"Uh oh, no go!"
"What if…"

Fearful / Fearless
Analysis / Intuition
Stuck / Flow

PEARL
Inner Strength:
"Try it."
"You'll be okay."
"You can handle it."
"Relax and release."
"So what, if…"

The concepts of EARL and PEARL epitomize the convergence of our heart-centered emotions, but what drives the physical manifestation of such feelings? The molecules of emotion percolating within our bustling heart center create a switchboard of communication that provides an amazing amount of information to our body and mind. As new science unfolds its many complexities, it becomes clear that our heart is an amazing organ, far more advanced than a simple blood-circulation pump.

Scientific pioneer Candace Pert, PhD, discovered the opiate receptor in the brain, and has demonstrated how tiny substances called neuropeptides play a huge role in our perceptions and emotional experiences. The exciting discovery of these neuropeptide compounds in the brain was soon followed by a rather surprising finding: neuropeptides are also located throughout the body and, in particular, clustered in the heart.[1] Much like a key fits into a lock, these small molecules carry information to cellular receptors, opening the doorway for a cascade of biological reactions to occur. The heart contains a copy of every single neuropeptide receptor found in the brain. The heart is also a major player in manufacturing and releasing these chemicals. These findings suggest that the heart, as well as the brain, is involved in information processing and emotional responses. The solid role the heart plays in keeping us alive and healthy complements its other possible role as caretaker of the spirit. It is no surprise that the remarkable heart is the first organ to form after conception and the last organ to shut down at death.

The Institute of HeartMath found that the heart sets a pace, an electric rhythm, for the entire body.[2] Although the brain is often considered the master organ, the heartbeat produces forty to sixty times more electrical amplitude than the brain. Every cell in the body is affected by the electrical signaling of the heart. Further, the heart's magnetic field is five thousand times greater than the field generated by the brain. It can even be detected several feet away from the body.

Besides its incredible electromagnetic capabilities, the heart is also a powerhouse of nerve cells. J. Andrew Armour, MD, PhD, one of the early pioneers in neurocardiology, introduced the concept of the "heart brain," describing the idea of an interacting yet independent nervous system in the heart.[3] This so-called brain in the heart encases forty thousand neurons that underpin the heart's ability, not only to process large amounts of information but also to sense, retain cellular memories, and learn. Indeed, the heart transmits more neurological information to the brain than the brain sends to the heart.[4]

Thus, the heart is a powerful entry point and master communicator that connects body, mind, emotion, and spirit. EARL and PEARL (or whatever you choose to call them) are your unique expressions of this complex network and the entryway for creating the balance needed to overcome worry, better manage emotions, and connect to inner peace.

GETTING UNSTUCK AND INTO FLOW

The heart beats about seventy times per minute. Each pump distributes nourishing blood throughout the body. When a blockage occurs, the entire system suffers damage. Our emotional energies can also suffer from blockages. We may flip-flop between being in flow (feeling powerful and that things are right) and being stuck (feeling worried, fearful, and ill at ease).

While in flow, things move along contentedly. However, when your emotions are stuck, pain has the upper hand. The good news is that pain serves a useful purpose: it makes you stop what you are doing. For example, when your hand comes near a flame, you feel pain and quickly withdraw your hand, protecting yourself from being burned.

Emotional pain does the same thing — it stops you from what you are doing. In order to protect you, EARL constantly monitors and creates judgments based on what you have learned. Thus, EARL chatters away, reiterating the beliefs you've developed. EARL pushes you to fear more in order to avoid possible injuries. On the other hand, PEARL provides guidance as to the beneficial aspects of a situation, showing you how to connect in a more positive way and to create safety.

Here's an example. You approach a puppy sitting on the sidewalk. EARL sees the dog as a possibly menacing creature that could snarl, bite, and harm. EARL wants you to avoid the dog. PEARL, however, sees a cute little puppy that would be fun to pet.

Which voice is right? You can't necessarily know unless you know the dog. Both are valid responses. *You* get to decide which one to choose based on other factors, such as: Does the dog behave as if it's afraid and might bite? Is it wagging its tail? Is it growling?

We need EARL to protect us. But we also need PEARL to help us expand beyond our fears. We need both aspects. They both help us. The problem is balance. If you've become stuck in worry, it means that you've tuned out PEARL and are instead allowing EARL to direct your life.

The first step in changing a worry-loaded lifestyle is to recognize these two inner forces, understand them, and choose which will direct your life. Although all problems do not magically dissolve, you can begin taking back control of your life by realizing that the power of choice is your ticket out of worry and fear. Your challenges may be the boost you need to create something better.

YOUR HIDDEN POWERS: AWARENESS AND CHOICE

How do you begin reconnecting with your fearless side? Simply become more aware of your thoughts and feelings. Instead of merely responding to life out of habit — especially if you're in the habit of listening to your EARL aspect — begin consciously choosing your reactions. Refuse to be the victim of your emotions; instead, become your own mental master by exercising your hidden power of choice.

When you are aware that you have choices, you become the leader of your thoughts, not the follower of your fears.

To better understand how your thoughts and feelings create your experience of life, consider the following example. It shows how we sometimes can let our stresses sour our outlook and seed more stress. It also shows how to perform a turnaround to make more productive choices in how we think and react to life.

Anna awakens on a Saturday morning to the sound of rain pounding against her bedroom window. Irritated, she pulls back the curtains to gaze outside. She had looked forward all week to gardening today. She immediately feels annoyed and thinks, "Stupid rain. This wasn't predicted. My plans are ruined."

She gets up, heads into the bathroom, peers into the mirror, and grumbles, "Oh my, I look so fat!"

Anna's thoughts and feelings are unconsciously telling her: "Today is awful, and I look terrible."

Anna continues her day in a bad mood and negative mindset. As she heads into the kitchen, she notices the living room is messy and thinks, "Look at this place. I cleaned it yesterday and now it's a mess. Why doesn't anybody pick up after themselves?"

Anna begins to feel even more irritated as she continues that train of thought with, "I'm the only one who ever does anything around here. What's their problem, anyway?"

Do you see what happened to Anna? She's not even aware of it, but after being up for only ten minutes, Anna programmed her day to begin with negativity, solely by her own thoughts and the reactions she chose to have toward each situation. How many stressful days began this way without Anna ever realizing it?

Let's rewind and see how Anna could choose to react differently to her experiences and dramatically change the outcome of her day.

Anna wakes up and hears rain on her bedroom window. Although she is disgruntled, she thinks, "Oh well, there are lots of other things I can do today rather than garden. Maybe I'll just relax. Besides, the rain will be good for the garden. Ahh, it's not so bad."

She strolls into the bathroom, glances into the mirror, squints, and puckers her lips, whimsically saying, "Hmm, you are one sexy babe."

As she walks into the kitchen, she notices the disheveled living room. She closes her eyes and thinks, "Hmm, if I could have one wish from the magic genie in the bottle, I would wish this room to be sparkling and beautiful . . . poof!" She opens her eyes, but nothing has changed, and she thinks, "Oh well, no genie maid today. I'll speak to the kids about this later. Cleanliness is next to godliness — and it's next to impossible too!"

Anna picks up a magazine she hasn't had time to read, pours a glass of orange juice, and watches the softly falling rain. She pops in a favorite CD and sits down to enjoy a peaceful moment.

Do you see the difference?

Your thoughts and feelings create your experience of life.

Learning how to better manage the everyday stresses that vex, annoy, and mangle our emotional well-being helps prevent a tense and worry-prone mindset. When you deal with your challenges, you feel empowered. When you set aside, ignore, or over-react to them, you weaken and chip away at your sense of well-being. A stress-filled life provides the fertile ground for the emergence of a tense and worried mind.

You always have choices. You can decide to focus on things that you like, rather than things you don't. You can lighten up and have a sense of humor. You can calmly and peacefully tackle a problem. It's not that you enjoy rescheduling your plans or being out of shape or having a messy house. You simply recognize your feelings and decide to do something other than feel angry, annoyed, or stressed. In this way, you observe your feelings for the input they provide, not absorb them to become immersed in the negativity.

These decisions have palpable consequences. Studies at the Institute of HeartMath found that the electromagnetic field produced by the heart becomes more coherent as the person shifts into a more loving or caring state.[5] Further, this electromagnetic information can be transmitted among individuals. Your heart can impact another's brain. When individuals touch or even are in close proximity, one person's electrocardiogram (EKG) signal is registered in the other person's electroencephalogram

(EEG). This signal is electromagnetic in origin, which suggests that we radiate energy to others.[6]

Thus, as we pay more attention to our thoughts and feelings, we can make better and more productive choices in how we react. This impacts not only us but also others around us.

You can *always* choose
to react differently.

You are not chained
to negative reactions.

You can do any number of things to create a happier and less worried state of mind by seeing situations differently. You can decide to connect with your PEARL side and feel peaceful, and release and redirect your EARL side that shouts with discontent.

You can also change your life to lovingly address aspects that need correction. Perhaps it's time to talk to the family about taking more responsibility for the house. Perhaps it's time to give up the mentality of "I take care of everything and everybody." Perhaps it's time to take action to get fit and trim. How you react is strictly up to you and no one else. Remember: You can't change life, but you can change your attitude toward it.

Sometimes our expectations or the inflexibility of our demands create stress and anxiety. Here's another example of how to put CORE concept 1 into practice.

John moved to a new home during the summer. His morning commute to work took about thirty minutes. His wife was a nurse at the local hospital and started work early and often worked overtime. John was in charge of getting the kids up, fed, and dressed, and driving them to daycare. As summer ended, schedules changed for the family. John would drop off the kids to elementary school and then head in to work. He noticed that traffic had become much more congested. He was late to work and to an early morning meeting. The next few days, he tried new ways to get to work in less time. He began timing small segments. "Hmm, that took seven minutes to get here and that shaved off about four minutes. Now, cutting through the park saves an additional three minutes unless the school buses go that way. Blast, the highway is backed up again!"

Day after day, John tried new routes, yet often arrived at work no faster — plus he was annoyed and had a headache. He worried about how many times he was barely on time or actually late. This was a new job. He wanted to keep making a good impression. What could he do? The kids had to be at school at a certain time, and only then could he head into work. He tried getting the kids up earlier and ready faster. That seemed to create more tension and stress for all. Then a light bulb came on. John realized he was focusing on what was worrying him and what was wrong — the kids' slowness in getting ready, the long commute and the traffic snarls, and being late. He thought, "What is it I really want? I want to arrive at work on time, enjoy my commute, and get the kids to school in a good frame of mind."

Instead of reacting with worry and anger, John realized that he had a choice. He could change how he was thinking about and responding to his daily schedule. He decided to open up to the other possibilities. As he began to do that, he found something interesting happening. By focusing on what he wanted, solutions appeared. He ran into his boss in the parking lot and they began a conversation about kids in school and getting to work on time. She suggested the possibility of starting a policy of flex time, as some of the other employees had similar problems.

The chance meeting led to a shift in company policy. John began to come in a little later, thus avoiding the traffic, and stayed a little longer. He also found out that the school had an afterschool program for parents who worked. The kids would go to the program immediately after school ended and he would pick them up later. Since the evening commute also had been unpredictable, this created just the solution he needed. Instead of feeling worried and stressed by focusing on the problem, he created solutions by focusing on what he wanted to see happen. Best of all, instead of spending the time worrying about whether he would be on time to get to work or pick up the kids, he could relax during the drive. His car became his temple of learning, as he played favorite audio books or listened to the radio.

John chose to transform his worries into solutions. Why? Because he found that while he couldn't control traffic, he could control his reaction to it, and by changing how he felt about the situation, new solutions appeared. John had many choices in how to more productively deal with this challenge. Once he became aware of that power, he used it to his benefit. He preferred to feel positive, happy, in flow, and content. Because of that fundamental shift in how he was thinking and reacting, John created a wonderfully positive solution.

To deal with worry and stress, you must recognize the absolute power of your thoughts. *You* are the one who accepts or rejects them. When you are worried, you are likely focusing on what's wrong about a situation. You are unconsciously accepting the negative thoughts of your EARL side. But you can also choose to soar past them by taking back control and redirecting your reactions.

Embrace PEARL. It's your power over worry and fear. Adjusting your unsettled mindset is a gradual process that begins by taking back control of your life and reformulating how you react to everyday stresses that seed so many of our worries.

WHAT YOU THINK ABOUT EXPANDS

Do you see how little thoughts can add up to big thoughts? Thoughts are like the air blown into a balloon.

What you think about expands.

Right now you may feel unhappy that your

worries seem to dominate your life. You may think that things will never get better. Let's stop filling up that balloon and choose another. To do so, you must first wake up inside. Mentally stretch and yawn. Begin examining your daily reactions. By understanding how you feel, you unleash the powerful tool of choice. This CORE concept helps you steer a different route than your autopilot is directing.

By recognizing and taking charge
of yourself, you can choose
peace instead of worry.

You take a giant leap into healing when you recognize your worries for what they are: feelings and thinking overwhelmed by EARL mentality. When you begin redirecting your reactions, you learn something valuable: how to recognize and embrace your PEARL side, the higher you who is powerful, energetic, and happy. You leave stress and worry in the dust.

At its innermost level, worry emerges because we are fearful about control and safety. As confusing as it may sound, the only true control lies in not demanding control. True control releases the need to control what is outside in favor of directing what is inside.

You jump-start this process by recognizing your internal power. You can't control the weather, a spouse who is irritable, or a child who acts unloving, but you do have control over how you think and react to all those things.

How we interact with others also offers a powerful means to better understand ourselves. Relationships can bless us with joy or ignite hurt. Here's a final example of how to put CORE concept 1 into practice.

Mary, a self-described worrywart, easily expressed happiness, but she paid little attention to her negative feelings. Her strategy was to deny them or just let them defuse over time. This was the way she had reacted since childhood, and it seemed like a normal thing to do.

The day before Mother's Day, she had a disagreement with her college-aged son and daughter about their money needs. Afterward, her EARL side fumed with righteous indignation and then boiled over. She felt angry, hurt, and unappreciated. As a single parent, she was putting them both through school with much financial sacrifice.

Inside, EARL tried to protect her by telling her she was being used and abused. This voice was loud and strong, and the quiet, balancing advice of PEARL paled in the fury. All of Mary's insecurities exploded as one hurtful thought led to the next. She could not bury these emotions or quickly defuse them. Deep down she worried about whether her children really loved her at all. She questioned whether she was even a good mother.

Mary churned the thoughts over all evening. The following morning, she was still worrying and overreacting. She abruptly canceled her Mother's Day lunch with her son and daughter — that would tell them how hurt she was. Since she felt terrible doing this, they would too, right?

Wrong. She brooded instead of resolving the issue. She did not feel at peace about her decision, but stuck with it anyway. That was an important signal from within that she hadn't yet learned to heed; she didn't realize that she was only punishing herself. Neither of her children understood her hurt feelings, because she never gave them the chance. She lost the opportunity to productively express her feelings, resolve the issues, and use the challenge to strengthen their bonds.

Although hurt, Mary had many choices

besides anger, rumination, and withdrawal. She could have chosen to use this situation as an opportunity to impose more reasonable limits on how much she was financing. After she cooled off, she could have discussed her hurt feelings with her children. She could have gotten some physical activity to help dissipate the bubbling emotions.

It is not easy being a parent, let alone one who is overly sensitive and easily hurt due to a very active EARL side. Mary's turning point came only after she began recognizing her power to *choose* other ways of dealing with hurts rather than the unproductive and stress-building tornados of negativity. Learning to distinguish between EARL and PEARL helped give her greater understanding and improved her interactions. Making better choices quelled the insidious buildup of stress that seeds and perpetuates worry and anxiety.

PRACTICE SOLVING, NOT STEWING

Expanding your PEARL side provides the key to productively responding to a negative situation. You must determine whether you feel peaceful about your responses and decisions. That is, are you coming from a place of love, fear, or anger? Your heart provides a living barometer to assess how you feel. Metaphysically, heaven and earth meet in the heart, which is both a physical and a spiritual bridge. There are three energy centers above and three energy centers below. We sense positive and negative reactions differently in the heart. Worry and anger both feel heavy. Love and peace feel full yet light. A heavy heart provides a red flag, signaling us that we are not approaching the situation from a place of love or peace; we may instead be coming out of the need to control others or the outside world. This can provide powerful input and guidance to alert us to the need to make a change.[7]

Jill Bolte Taylor, PhD, a brain scientist, has illustrated the very predictable responses our bodies have to worry, anxiety, and fear.[8] The neuronal loop circuits can cause a variety of physiological changes such as tightness in the chest, shallow breathing, lightheadedness, stomach upset, jiggling legs, and so on. These are predictable responses that last initially about ninety seconds. That is your window of opportunity to cancel, instead of continue, the emotional response. Once alerted to such emotional responses, you can wait ninety seconds for it to die down and then begin to ask your brain to react differently. By acknowledging the ability of your brain to think the thoughts and feel the emotions while insisting that you are really not interested in thinking those thoughts and feelings anymore, you can maintain control of automatic reactions that are not coming from a place of love. Observe the feelings for the input they provide, but do not absorb them and become immersed in the negativity.

Another strategy for dealing with a heavy heart and troubling emotions is to, again, acknowledge their presence, but then focus on someone or something you *love*. By changing your feelings, you change your chemistry. This gives you time to develop a more peaceful solution to your challenges. For example, instead of feeling worried and troubled about an interaction you had with someone else, focus instead on a fond memory of your favorite pet, your loving mate, or some pleasant moment of peace. Dwell intently within the moment. Remember and soak up the emotions as fully as you can. Return to this place of peace and love if negative emotions return. By doing this practice, you place your intentions on love, increasing your positive energy, encouraging your intuitive guidance, and providing more for you to feel positive about. Try it!

Are you willing to become more aware of how your internal dialogues seed worry and anxiety? Are you willing to exercise your ability to veto such reactions? Here's one powerful way to do it. Practice *solving* — not *stewing.*

Don't worry if you initially lapse into old habits. It's far easier in the beginning to fall back than it is to forge forward. Establishing new ways of thinking and reacting requires time, patience, and practice, practice, practice. And, oh yes, did I mention practice? But as these new skills develop, your sense of peace and happiness builds. As you empower yourself to express your feelings productively, you take a giant leap into a happier life and into wonderful new dimensions in your relationships with others.

Understanding that you do indeed have choices provides authentic power and guides your first steps into learning better ways of responding. By recognizing and simply observing how your inner dialogues affect your mood and behavior, you launch your journey out of automatic negative thinking. You can choose peace instead of worry.

Recovery from worry is a journey,
not a destination.

Take your first step into better managing your worries and living a more empowered life. Write the following on a piece of paper and post it where you can see it daily:

I always have choices.

While the remainder of this book provides tips, tools, and strategies for overcoming the worried mindset, here's a sneak preview for how to worry smart.

TEN WAYS TO WORRY SMART

1. *Create a power phrase.* Tell yourself that "This too shall pass!" or "All is well." Remind yourself of how past worries seldom came true. Text or email yourself a helpful quote or phrase for encouragement.
2. *Keep calm and carry on.* Focus on now and practice under-reacting as a means of countering automatic tendencies to over-react.
3. *Postpone worrying — or set a future time to consider issues.* At night, say, "There is nothing more I can do about this problem tonight, so I'll deal with it tomorrow."

4. *Write about your worries.* Journal about your current worries and possible solutions to them.
5. *Imagine the best-case scenario.* Visualize things going the way you want, and how happy you will feel about it.
6. *Plan for how you will handle negative outcomes.* Prepare a response for several possible scenarios.
7. *Exercise.* Exercising is an all-natural antidepressant and tension reducer.
8. *Spend time quietly relaxing or out in nature.* They don't call it Mother Nature for nothing. Placing your feet on the ground actually helps ground your energies.
9. *Smile! Take it all less seriously and less personally.* Studies show that whether you mean it or not, smiling releases mood-enhancing endorphins.
10. *Take a worry-free day at least once a week!* Like the sound of Worry-Free Wednesdays? The more you practice, the easier it becomes. You may find it feels so good that you'll make it an everyday practice.

Chapter Summary
- Your feelings define, empower, and direct your journey through life.
- Recovery from worry and anxiety begins

symbolically at the level of the heart when you learn to accept and understand your thoughts and feelings.

- We consist of higher and lower aspects. These are not good or bad, but are like two poles of a magnet. One attracts and one repels. Your higher self feels connected, happy, loving, creative, energetic, and powerful. Your lower self feels worried, angry, hostile, and fearful.
- Your thoughts and reactions tip the balance between living in higher or lower emotions.
- Activating choice fuels authentic power.
- Your thoughts and feelings create your experience of life. What you think about expands.
- You can't always change what happens to you, but you can always choose your attitude.
- You can use your power of conscious intention to choose peace instead of worry.
- Decide to become the leader of your thoughts, not the follower of your fears.

The Plan:
Implement CORE Concept 1

Start keeping a personal journal, and on the first page write: "I always have choices."

During the next week, become more aware of how you can make better choices that leave you feeling happy and peaceful instead of worried, angry, and upset. Record some of your thoughts, feelings, and reactions. You don't have to list every thought you are having — some say we think 100,000 thoughts a day — but the goal is to realize you are making choices all the time. Notice how your thoughts make you feel, and play with the idea of improving your choices. Don't make a judgment as to whether your thoughts are good or bad, right or wrong; just observe them and experiment with the idea of changing your reactions.

Try It

Make three columns:

My Feelings/ Thoughts	My Beliefs	Productive Changes

List things that have upset you. Dig down and find out how your thoughts and beliefs contributed to those feelings. Recognize that these are choices you are making. Next, experiment with the idea of changing how you think and react to better deal with negative reactions. Choose to see them from another angle. Write three ways you can react differently to the situation. Empower yourself by developing ideas for how you could react in a way that gives you a more positive, peaceful feeling.

For example, consider the example of the annoyances with traffic. For the first column, you could write: "I am feeling annoyed and angry about traffic." In the second column, you could write: "My inner belief is that I don't have any control over this, and it wastes my valuable time." In the third column, you could write: "I can choose to use this time more enjoyably. I recognize the traffic, but I don't choose to focus on it. I can choose a more scenic route. I can play my personal-growth recordings or listen to music. I can choose to enjoy the commute."

EVALUATE
After you've done this for a week, write a summary of what happened when you tried

to change your reactions. Did you like the exercise? Did changing your attitude help you delve into the many thoughts that you experience during a day? Are you getting better at noticing your thoughts, feelings, and reactions? Are you beginning to make more productive choices in how you react and exercise your veto power over negativity? Step back into a more powerful and peaceful life by making regular entries in your journal.

Notes

1. Candace Pert, *Molecules of Emotion: The Science Behind Mind-Body Medicine* (New York: Simon & Schuster, 1999).
2. For more than twenty years, the Institute of HeartMath (www.heartmath.org) has studied physiologic mechanisms of communication between the heart and brain and how those interactions critically drive our perceptions, emotions, and health.
3. J. Andrew Armour, "The Little Brain on the Heart," *Cleveland Clinic Journal of Medicine* 74, Supplement 1 (2007): 848–851.
4. Paul Pearsall, *The Heart's Code: Tapping the Wisdom and Power of Our Heart Energy* (New York: Broadway Books, 1998). In

The Heart's Code Dr. Pearsall, a transplant surgeon, wrote about cellular memory in transplant patients. He described many cases in which transplant recipients often initially seemed to have the memories and even personality features of the person whose heart they received.

5. Rollin McCraty, Mike Atkinson, William A. Tiller, Glen Rein, and Alan D. Watkins, "The Effects of Emotions on Short-Term Power Spectrum Analysis of Heart Rate Variability," *American Journal of Cardiology* 76, no. 14 (1995): 1089–1093. The key findings of this study show us that different emotions affect autonomic nervous system function and balance in measurably different ways. Anger tends to increase sympathetic activity (i.e. fight or flight), while appreciation is associated with a relative increase in parasympathetic activity (i.e. calming).

6. Rollin McCraty, *The Energetic Heart: Bioelectromagnetic Interactions within and between People* (Boulder Creek, CA: Institute of HeartMath, 2008). Chapter 35 in *Bioelectromagnetic Medicine,* Paul J. Rosch and Marko S. Markov, eds., (New York: Marcel Dekker, 2004): 541–562. The key findings from this study show us that when two people are at a conversa-

tional distance, the electromagnetic signal generated by one person's heart can influence the other person's brain rhythms. When an individual is generating a coherent heart rhythm, synchronization between that individual's brainwaves and another person's heartbeat is more likely to occur.

7. Marci Shimoff, *Love for No Reason: 7 Steps to Creating a Life of Unconditional Love* (New York: Free Press, 2010). In this book, Shimoff describes the significance of our heart's reaction in helping us to understand our emotions.

8. Jill Bolte Taylor, *My Stroke of Insight: A Brain Scientist's Personal Journey* (New York: Viking, 2008).

■ ■ ■ ■ ■

CORE CONCEPT 2:
I CHOOSE TO
CHANGE MY
OUTLOOK

■ ■ ■ ■ ■

4
How You Think About Anything Determines How You Experience Everything

Our mental commentary influences and colors our feelings and perceptions about what's going on in our lives, and it is these thought forms that ultimately attract and create everything that happens to us.
— Shakti Gawain

As you become more aware of the thoughts constantly bubbling in your head, you may be surprised by how many negative ones appear. How often do you feel helpless, blocked, fearful, or unhappy? Don't worry if you notice this type of pattern. You are in the process of discovery.

Now it's time to focus on the turnarounds for negative thoughts and construct a new, more powerful mindset. By drawing on your ability to consciously focus your intentions, you can create solutions that turn your worries into opportunities instead of possible catastrophes. In other words, what you think about you can bring about. CORE concept 2 is:

I choose to change my outlook.

You likely feel unhappy and upset about many things right now — and one of them is you. Every time you begin to overworry, you are experiencing a crisis of confidence. You feel powerless and unable to resolve what is happening to you. You worry, mope, and stuff your feelings down. But what if you can turn those thoughts around? What if you can feel powerful instead of fearful? What if you knew you could handle anything that came along? What if you were your own safety net and strength?

When you learn to emotionally depend on and take care of yourself, you take a giant leap out of worry and fear. You become the leader of your thoughts, not the follower of your fears. If you are aware of your thoughts and feelings, you can exert your power over them by choosing to react differently. You rewire circuits blown by overworrying and negativity by using a new type of wire, one constructed of positive images and conscious intentions.

HOW TO TALK TO YOURSELF: CREATING MANIFESTOS

To begin rewiring these circuits, you need to first formulate a plan that directs your thinking on a regular basis, using positive statements and mental imagery to create desired changes in your life. Some people refer to these as affirmations and visualizations. I simply call them "Say-So" manifestos. What you mentally say can make it so. In other words, directing how you talk to yourself helps create or manifest what you want. The ultimate goal is to feel powerful instead of fearful. You begin the process of changing your outlook by creating your own manifestos that counteract and challenge worry and negative statements.

What do you do with a pair of shoes that are worn out and old? You replace them with a new pair, but they have to be the right size. The same is true with your old, worn-out negative thinking. For your journey out of worry and fear, you need to begin with a good-fitting pair of new boots.

These new boots are your Say-So manifestos. When you put them on, you hike along a different path. Here, as you recognize negative thoughts, you throw them out and consciously replace them. There are four basic steps to this powerful process I call the Four Ps. You create statements that are:

- Powerful
- Positive
- Present tense
- Possibilizing

These statements challenge negativity and worry, and replace them with something that you want — but also something you can believe. I call this "possibilizing" because in some place within you, however remote it feels now, lies a bounty of possibilities for a life that is happier and more powerful.

How are *you* choosing to see yourself and your life now? Try this exercise. Get a pencil and a piece of paper. On the left side of your paper, write the negative feelings that are percolating within you. These are the bad vibes that keep you feeling powerless. On the right side of your paper, counter each negative thought by writing (in the present tense) a more powerful, positive possibility.

Here are some examples:

WEAKENING THOUGHTS	EMPOWERING MANIFESTOS
I feel helpless.	I am strong and capable.
I am stupid.	I am intelligent and have a great personality.
I can't stop worrying.	I choose to change my life now.
I shouldn't feel like this.	My attitude is my choice.
I can't trust myself.	I am the leader of my thoughts.
I feel overwhelmed by everything.	I am powerful and loving.

Can you sense the differences in how the first set of thoughts makes you feel versus the second? As you write each empowering manifesto, check to see that it follows the Four Ps. Ask yourself these questions as you write:

• Is it powerful or weak? Did you use strong words?
• Is it positive or negative? There is a big difference between saying "I don't want to be weak" as opposed to "I am strong and

capable." The latter focuses on the positive.

- Is it in the present tense? That is, does it use phrases such as "I am" or "I now choose"? If you say, "I want to be strong and capable," you're saying you're *not* strong and capable right now. To ignite this type of energy and make it work for you, phrase your manifesto as if it were true now, such as "I am strong and capable."
- Can you possibilize about this? Even if you don't feel powerful or capable right now, is it a possibility? Can you believe your statements?

Fuel Your Statements with Feelings

Focusing your mind on powerful statements and focused intentions helps draw such energies to you. But to make them even more powerful, do one other thing: Add some real punch to your list by imagining what it would feel like to live out each idea. That is, see yourself fully immersed in it. Experience your vision and really get into the image.

Focus on You

You cannot control others or cause them to do something they don't wish to do. Rather, you are changing yourself and the circumstances of your own life.

Be Open

Focus on *how* you want to feel and not *when* you want it to happen. Time is something we cannot control. What happens may manifest itself differently than the way you imagined. Focusing on the *feeling you wish to create* allows it to show up in a thousand different ways. Allow things to flow naturally and in their own way. Remain open to all possibilities.

You have now created a template to begin living a more empowered life that focuses on happiness in the present, not worry and fear of the future. By crafting a new set of responses to automatic inner trash talk, you begin to step out of negativity and worry. But this requires endurance and determination. Remember:

Patience, perseverance, and practice
propel you forward and engage the
manifesting gears of the universe.

No longer are you adrift in a sea of worry. Now, with conscious projection and focused intention, you create the necessary energy to follow a life path of joy and inner peace, ready to fulfill your destiny.

Create your own manifesto. Own it, feel it, and change it at any time:

- Patience, perseverance, and practice propel me forward.
- I move in synchronicity with my life.
- I create joy wherever I am.
- I am guided and always have access to help.
- I create my own inner peace.

Flood your mind with thoughts that reflect the way you now want to think and react. Read your manifestos at least three times daily: once in the morning, once during the day, and once before you go to sleep. Each time, take a moment to feel inside and try to become what you've written. Change or tweak them if you desire, but keep the statements private. Only you need to see them. If someone else sees them and comments negatively, let it pass. Their inability to understand is their problem, not yours.

Here's a word of caution: Do not create manifestos with ideas you cannot even remotely believe. For example, unless you are a genius, don't tell yourself, "I am smarter than Albert Einstein." If you are as smart as Al, then go for it. But there are lots of other legitimate possibilities you could focus on when you possibilize. It is better to say things like "I am intelligent and capable," "I am fit and trim" (if you are planning on getting that way), or "I am strong and healthy." You could also say "I am insightful and talented" or "I have a great personality."

Remember, the goal is to take something that is a possibility and see it as a reality. Fantasizing is its own reward. Possibilizing isn't the same as denying negative feelings. Everyone has them. You simply work to overcome automatic negativity by seeing things differently.

Get off of your negative autopilot and on to some fun. Enjoy this process. Few things in life are really as serious as we tend to make them. I have been known to look into the mirror and say, "Darling, you look marvelous!" Then I smile, hold my head high, point my nose to the ceiling, and shake my round tummy. I refuse to take myself so seriously. Whimsy can be wonderful!

Some people say, "Fake it till you make it," which is fine as long as what you are imagining is something you can believe in. Possibilizing is a powerful way of changing your life and creating a happier you who feels more in control.

What we say or hear can have powerful effects on us because there is a part of our mind that cannot distinguish between what is real and what is imaginary. Some compare it to programming a computer. A computer doesn't decide. It only spits back what it was programmed to do. Obviously, we humans are a lot more complicated than computers, but in some ways we are amazingly similar. So, for example, if we act confidently and really want to become confident, we may become so if we focus on that intention. We are reprogramming ourselves.

As a child, Brenda Fraser was the quiet one, the youngest of six children. Her mother had a doll representative of each of her daughters. While cute, the doll representing Brenda did not have a marking or stitching to indicate a mouth. That's because Brenda seemed to have no voice, as she stayed out of the family fights and drama. She kept to herself and seldom spoke up. Growing up, she was somewhat shy and introspective, writing poetry and listening to the radio alone in her room.

As a young woman in college and in the years thereafter, she worried every time she had to give a presentation in front of a class or a group of any kind. She dreaded the day and wondered how would she do and if she could overcome her nervousness and discomfort when she was giving her presentation. Her physical symptoms didn't help. Her heart would race and she would feel sick to her stomach and shaky as she anticipated the day.

In her early thirties, Brenda got a job as the executive assistant to the chairman of the US Holocaust Memorial Museum in Washington, DC. This was an important job that required leading tours and giving remarks on the museum's auditorium stage in front of four hundred people.

Despite her worries and trepidation, Brenda realized she needed to change her outlook and reprogram her thoughts about speaking in public. In her job, she met many inspiring people who were amazing examples of triumph over adversity. Holocaust survivors told her their stories of survival and forgiveness; they shared the profound losses they suffered and the complete destruction of all they knew. By learning humility from these survivors and thinking about what's really important and what a special gift life is, Brenda was able to overcome her worry and fear of public speaking. She learned to challenge and face her fears.

Brenda made a decision to view speaking differently. Instead of worrying what people might think of her, she began to focus on the bigger purpose of the talk. Rather than getting tripped up about following a script word for word, she realized it was more important to just speak from her heart. She could convey important information and also provide a personal story to illustrate a point. When giving a presentation or speech, she would simply ask herself, "How can I be of service to my listeners? Can I rely on my Higher Power to help me?" She learned to heed the inner voice that said, "Just trust that the words will come through you."

Brenda says that everyone has a story to tell that contains a key message to someone else who is hurting, confused, or needing inspiration. By challenging her inner critic, by disagreeing with the internal voice of doubt, Brenda learned to allow inspiration to flow.

Today, Brenda speaks professionally and has her own weekly internet show, viewed by thousands all over the globe. Her goal is to help people thrive by sharing success tips, showcasing individuals who have overcome their own fears and obstacles, and giving hope.

Not bad for a child who seldom spoke up.

Whether you realize it or not, buried within you is a beautiful, intelligent, talented, and loving spirit. This spirit may feel squashed or held back by circumstances, upbringing, or automatic self-defeating thoughts. When you create manifestos, you are simply borrowing a trait that you would like to tug to the surface from your higher self.

Begin today to practice seeing yourself differently. Indulge yourself in the possibility that you are someone who is powerful and who is making positive changes in your life. Get mad at negativity, and toss it out the door. As you continue to practice seeing yourself in this way, you will begin to notice the powerful effects of self-directed, positive thoughts. In this frame of mind, worry no longer dominates your life.

IT DOESN'T HAVE TO BE PERFECT

Don't worry if you initially struggle to turn around your negative thinking. You are in practice mode. Just try it on a regular basis. The more you work on transforming your outlook, the better you become at turning off negativity and turning on possibility.

What if you have trouble figuring out how to counter negativity? Pretend that your best friend or your child is feeling negative. How would you advise them?

Always worrying and assuming the worst might happen stalls the energy of creation. Use your wonderful powers of imagination to visualize only the best possible outcome. Each time you find yourself worrying about potential problems, simply change those thoughts with practice, practice, practice.

I found that an amazing thing happened to me as I energized my authentic power and forged a stronger connection to my inner spirit. I began to experience some rather cool coincidences. One of my best manifestos came to me by accident.

At the time, I was working on a National Institutes of Health grant application to fund a research project. I had finished my experiments at the lab and decided to go home to write in peace and quiet.

As I worked on my home computer, I began to feel bogged down by trying to plan complicated experiments that would be done in the future. Much of science is experiential in that you must first try something, and only after you see the results can you plan the next step. In any event, I decided to stop and turn on the television for a brief break.

A talk show host was interviewing an entertainer who earned her living by singing at gigs around the country. At one point, the host asked the entertainer if she missed her home, since she was on the road for so much of the year. The entertainer smiled, thought about it briefly, and said, "You know, honey, my home is in my belly button. I take it with me wherever I go."

I can't remember the rest of the interview, but those words stuck with me. That's exactly how I wanted to feel — peaceful no matter where I might travel. From that day on, I added a new manifesto to my growing arsenal: "My home is in my belly button. My safety and security are within me."

I later added, "Wherever I go, that's where I am" to remind me that "Wherever I am, I'm safe." I was programming myself to realize and believe that I can feel safe anywhere; I can take care of myself and feel calm and peaceful.

By harnessing the power of focused intention, we can create a vision first in our mind and then watch how it manifests. Challenging our automatic lapses into negativity requires patience, time, and the belief that our dreams are possible.

You know who are experts at manifestos? Olympic athletes. To succeed at the highest level of athletic competition, these athletes must have talent, but they must also perform robust physical training and focused mental conditioning. They must overcome their own fears of failing.

Take the story of two-time Olympic Gold Medalist Cathy Turner, who is one of only three people ever to win gold medals in consecutive Winter Olympic Games.[1] Her career total of four medals ranks fourth for most medals ever won by a Winter Olympian.

When she was seven, Cathy used to climb into a big chair in front of a mirror in her parents' bedroom and victoriously wave her arms above her head in slow motion. She was pretending she had just crossed the finish line after winning first place in speed skating.

She skated most of her life. It was a natural talent. She tried out for the 1980 Olympic team and just missed making it.

She was heartbroken. Despondent, she decided to quit skating altogether. She then pursued and achieved a successful music career. But several years later, she became severely depressed. Something was missing from her life.

One morning while sitting in her kitchen, Cathy happened to read an article in the newspaper about a former teammate who was training for the Olympics. She instantly realized that what she really wanted most was to pursue her goal of competing in the Olympics. Cathy's mother encouraged her to pursue her dream. Cathy called her former coach, who suggested she come and train with them.

She had no skates and no money. She was also older and out of shape. The other athletes jokingly called her "grandma." But she persisted with her vision. She focused and believed in her dream. She trained hard, used imagery, and made the team.

As the Olympics approached, a strange thing began happening in her head. When visualizing the 500-meter race, she pictured herself in the lead, but suddenly two bigger girls would pass her by and cross the finish line before her. Each time she tried to envision her race, this same scene popped up again and again. She felt confused and upset. She was worrying about possible catastrophes.

Cathy decided to tackle the issues brought up by the voice of worry. Instead of avoiding the disturbing thoughts, she decided to ponder why she was experiencing such a gripping worry. As she examined her feelings, she realized that these competitors represented her own fears of losing.

She remembered how disappointed her father was whenever she lost and how pleased it made him when she won. She realized that when she focused on pleasing her father, instead of pleasing herself, she began to worry about losing. This mindset was crippling her dreams.

Cathy also recognized another thing. She was in the driver's seat in her mental race. She decided to accept and deal with her fear of failing, and she focused on the higher advice of her PEARL aspect. Cathy knew that her strength emanated from within herself.

She decided to restructure her vision by focusing on how she felt about herself and not worrying about her father's approval or disapproval. By changing her outlook, she accepted and dealt with her worry head-on. She also focused on the idea that she was going to race anyway, so she could either worry about losing and dwell on the negatives or look forward to competing and, if needed, learn from her mistakes.

These changes popped the bubble of worry and allowed Cathy to be the Olympic competitor she envisioned herself to be. The next time she visualized her race and saw the girls start to pass her, she just extended the track to make the race last a little longer — and she easily passed them. This put her in control again and helped fuel the confidence she needed to bring her to the track on February 24, 1992.

As she waited at the starting line that morning, Cathy found a bad edge on her left skate that could make her slip on the turns. Also, a false start caused her to fall hard onto the ice, bruising her hip and soaking her uniform. Everything seemed to be going wrong, not at all how she had envisioned it.

But her mental training paid off. She had become good at changing her outlook. Instead, she again focused on what she wanted to happen. Soaked and hurting, she dug in and mentally said, "I'm ready. Let's fly!"

The gun sounded. Off she went, but in

second place. As the girls flew around the turn, China's top skater, Yan Li, and two other athletes were neck and neck and ahead of Cathy. But Cathy remained focused. When the opportunity presented itself, she zoomed past all of them.

As they were approaching the finish line, Yan Li crept up on Cathy's inside and they accidentally clicked skates, causing Cathy to slow down and lose some ground. The finish line was up ahead. Seconds later, Yan leaned forward to cross the finish line. Cathy's body instantly reacted and she too surged forward, neck and neck with Yan. For precious moments, no one knew who had won. Then the scoreboard flashed the results. Cathy had beaten Yan by 4/100ths of a second and won the Olympic Gold Medal!

From atop the awards platform, Cathy raised her arms and joyfully waved to the crowd. The view was everything she had imagined when she was just a little girl, standing on her parents' oversized chair. She also went on to win medals when she competed in two more Olympics, in 1994 and 1998.

Cathy knew that our biggest limitations are the worries in our own minds. Once we understand and deal with them, we can do anything. She felt inside that there are no limits, and that if you can see it and believe it, you can be it. She changed her outlook.

Instead of worrying about possible negative outcomes, she focused on the feeling of triumph.

Some people say "I'll believe it when I see it," but those who truly understand how to make their dreams a reality know that the reverse is true: when you see it, you will believe it! As writer Ambrose Redmoon said:

"Courage is not the absence of fear, but rather the judgment that something else is more important than fear."

Change your outlook to one that focuses not on the absence of worry, but on what is most important: the possible positive outcomes and the feelings of victory, joy, and success.

If you want to overcome the worries blocking you and run your own race, you can't do it solely by thinking positively. Say-So manifestos involve a process of exploring, discovering, and changing your attitudes and beliefs. They guide your thinking, replace limitations, and create life as you wish, first on the inside — the true source of your authentic power.

Chapter Summary

- Dealing positively with worry involves more than just not feeling afraid or concerned about the future. It means changing your outlook and the way you think about yourself and your life.
- To change your outlook, create positive images and statements to guide how you want to think.
- Manifestos redirect negative and fearful thinking.
- Manifestos counteract and challenge negative thoughts.
- Manifestos are:

  - Powerful
  - Positive
  - Present tense
  - Possibilizing

- When you can see it and believe it, you can be it!
- You can choose power instead of worry.

New Strategies: Clear Your Clutter
THE PLAN

Set the stage for positive changes by cleaning out some of the clutter in your life. This symbolic gesture gets energy moving by tossing out old stuff (your worries and limitations) and making room for the new. It's time to unclutter and take charge.

TRY IT

Find an area that is cluttered. It can be a closet, cupboard, or your desk. It's time to get rid of the old, worn out, and unused stuff. Embrace a new you. You are now more powerful and in control of your own life. Organize your belongings. Get rid of clothes you haven't worn in more than a year, books and magazines you don't need to keep, and paperwork cluttering your space. Be ruthless. Give away, sell, or toss what you don't need or use.

EVALUATE

When you are all done, consider how this process made you feel. Doesn't taking charge of your own stuff and getting organized feel empowering? Use this experiment as a beginning and symbolic step for cleaning out the emotional clutter in your spirit. Ralph Waldo Emerson said:

"Finish each day and be done with it.
You have done what you could.
Some blunders and absurdities no doubt

135

crept in.
Forget them as soon as you can.
Tomorrow is a new day; you shall begin it
well and serenely."

Note

1. John Naber, *Awaken the Olympian Within: Stories from America's Greatest Olympic Motivators* (Santa Ana, CA: Griffin Publishing Group, 2000).

5
OUTLOOK MAKEOVER: TERRIBILIZING VERSUS POSSIBILIZING

You can't solve a problem with the same mind that created it.

— Albert Einstein

CORE concept 1 (*I Always Have Choices*) helped you energize two powerful tools for taking charge of your life: awareness and choice. By first becoming aware of how your thinking can keep you stuck in worry, you choose to step out of it and take another path. CORE concept 2 (*I Choose to Change My Outlook*) showed some specific ways to become the leader of your thoughts, not the follower of your fears.

This chapter and the next two build on and expand CORE concept 2 by showing you three powerful strategies to eliminate inner trash talk and take charge of your life. I call these "Outlook Makeovers" because they are interior transformations. This new mental grooming replaces the harried and worried you with a new peaceful and powerful you. Let's focus now on the ways you can stop the automatic terribilizing that seeds and perpetuates your chronic worrying.

THE HABIT OF TERRIBILIZING

Much of our behavior and thinking is so automatic that we aren't aware of how we are reacting; we just do it. The problem comes when automatic thoughts turn us into a churning stress factory. Understanding these natural tendencies allows us to steer clear of unproductive patterns of behavior.

You are making a choice when you feel worried and upset. You are agreeing with the inner voice that shouts, "Oh no, this is awful; this is terrible." When you are afraid about the unknown future and obsess about bad things that might happen, you have chosen to terribilize without knowing it. You have decided to think that something is or could become terrible.

Terribilizing is an energy-draining habit that hardwires your brain into a state of chronic worry, stress, and anxiety. The good news is that you can learn to make other choices once you see how you are automatically choosing to terribilize without ever knowing it. You may have started terribiliz-ing because of something that has happened to you. In this case, both memory and anticipation seed further worry.

There is a Swedish proverb that says, "Worry gives a small thing a big shadow."

When you are in the shadow of your wor-ries, you may not see the "sun" — the solu-tion to your problem. When you are in the shadow of your worries, you focus on what's wrong, not on what's right. When you are in the shadow of your worries, you stall creative energies and block your intuitive guidance.

EMOTIONAL HANGOVERS: SENSITIZED TO WORRYING

Our minds can quickly and automatically imbibe a stream of negative worry thoughts, and the result can be an emotional hangover in which negative energy remains in our minds. Because we have created this nega-tive habit, we may also believe this familiar response is somehow helping us to deal with our challenges. That is, perhaps we hope on some level that worry is protecting us from possible upsetting or challenging situations. We may believe that worry gives us a neces-sary buffer, helping us to prepare for pos-sible problems.

Such was the case for Margie. For many years, a show called "Sesame Street Live" would come to Saint Louis in mid-January. Another frequent visitor in January was snowy and inclement weather. Each year, Margie wanted to take her children to the show, but she worried that a snow- or ice storm could occur at the same time. Having to travel in such inclement weather worried her. Margie thought, "Why should I buy tickets that I might not be able to use?" However, Margie's niece faithfully bought tickets each year, packed up her own kids, and headed into the city. Some years later, Margie discussed this with her niece, who remarked that nine out of ten performances had been on easily drivable days.

How many times has worry kept you from doing what you wanted? Margie says she now realizes that worrying about bad weather that never happened robbed her of many opportunities to share fun experiences with her children.

Many of us do the same thing; we spend time ruminating about something that never occurs. Even when it doesn't stop us from doing something, we waste too much energy worrying about and planning for a terrible situation that seldom materializes.

OUR TERRIBLE/WONDERFUL PERSONALITIES

Our worry-filled minds can get caught in scary thought patterns. Unless we become aware of how we think, we quickly become stuck. We can worry and obsess over anything. We are expert terribilizers. We have the type of highly reactive personalities that take everything seriously and personally. We also feel responsible for everyone and every situation.

Do a little self-inventory. Do you tend to overworry, overreact, overdramatize, overcriticize, or become overly sensitive? If so, it's likely that you tend to terribilize. When you choose to terribilize, you choose the path of worry and fear. However, it is also just as likely that you are creative, talented, compassionate, and intelligent.

This is a package deal that blends both sets of energies. For example, the same kind of person who gets hurt easily because they are overly sensitive may also be a sympathetic and caring friend. The mind that fears catastrophes is also the same mind that makes you an imaginative artist, colorful writer, witty conversationalist, or creative problem-solver. These characteristics place

141

you among a select group of individuals. Elaine Aron, PhD, suggests that 15 to 20 percent of all people have highly sensitive personalities.[1] The scientific term for this distinct personality trait is "sensory-processing sensitivity." It is an innate feature of many organisms, from fruit flies to people. Those who are highly sensitive have nervous systems that not only pick up much more sensory information but also have increased sensitivity to stress and can be more easily overwhelmed. Highly sensitive children may overreact to and fear loud noises. Highly sensitive adults may feel sensory overload in certain circumstances. Despite a biological predisposition to over-react, a better understanding of such features allows us to temper, moderate, and use these traits to our best advantage.

No matter what personality type you are, chronic worrying is still a choice you are making. To choose differently, it is time to begin formulating a plan. Decide to change those automatic inner dialogues that hold you back and keep you stuck; choose not to terribilize. Terribilizing is a *learned* way of handling stressors. It combines your natural tendencies with inner dialogues that origi-nate in an internal echo chamber. But you possess both free will and veto power.

THE ECHO CHAMBER

All of us have an internal mental chamber filled with echoes of what we have heard others say to us, about us, and then ultimately what we say to ourselves. What is in your echo chamber? When you terribilize, it means you are a worrier, with echoes containing many "I'm nots" and "I can'ts," such as:

I'm not capable.
I'm not smart enough.
I'm not thin enough.
I'm not talented enough.
I'm not attractive enough.
I'm not deserving.
I'm not lovable.
I can't do it.
I can't have what I want.
I can't get what I need.
I can't trust myself.
I can't handle this.

When our echo chambers are reverberating with these self-limiting messages, we naturally worry and terribilize. After all, if your mind is squawking *I can't handle this,* then of course you worry, *What if I can't handle this?* When you hear *You're not good enough,* that eventually translates into *I'm not good enough.* Those thoughts rob you of your power and propel you into feeling that you may not be capable of solving your challenges.

Where did these echoes come from? They originate from many sources, such as family, teachers, friends, and acquaintances. Everyone has his or her own echo chamber. Remember: What people believe about themselves, they often unknowingly project onto others. So if they are being judgmental, they often accuse others of being so.

When you don't feel good enough, you send that message to others. In other words, you are thinking, *I'm not good enough,* and it comes out as "You aren't good enough" to someone else. Conversely, if you feel good about yourself, you are more supportive of other people as well.

Other messages that fill our echo chambers come from television, movies, and music. When you see skinny, glamorous models, you may tend to think, *To be attractive you have to be thin, thin, thin. I'm not thin, so I'm not attractive.*

Echoes have a curious side effect. When you hear them often enough, you begin to believe they are true, and your inner voice ultimately copies them. What thoughts are bouncing around your echo chamber? And more importantly, do you accept them or not? If your mind is filled with these thoughts, it's time to rewire terribilizing into possibilizing.

WORRY REMEDY: POSSIBILIZING

Instead of keeping your autopilot set on terribilizing, you can shift gears. We've already discussed the power of possibilizing as a means to create manifestos for a more balanced mindset. Now, it's time to focus on possibilizing as a specific antidote to the worry that creeps in from terribilizing.

You can cancel automatic terribilizing by offering yourself alternatives that emphasize positive possibilities. In other words, isn't it possible that the worst disaster will not happen and things will be fine? Possibilizing counters worried and stress-building thoughts. It emphasizes, *What if I can?*

One afternoon after work, I stopped by the grocery store to pick up a few items. As I got out of my car, I caught sight of a young woman unsteadily pushing a grocery cart. As she stepped, one leg came up higher than the other, while her head bobbed to the side.

I realized she had a physical disability. I wondered if she would be able to make it to the disabled parking spot where she was heading or if I should dart over to see if she needed any help. She steadfastly proceeded to her nearby car, placed the bags one by one into the trunk and then returned the cart.

My concerns about whether she might need help were quickly answered as she got into her car and proceeded to drive away. As her car turned to head out of the lot, I noticed her license plate. It read: CAN DO. This young woman is a bona fide possibilizer who focuses on the positives, not the negatives.

If you look around, you find there are lots of possibilizers out there with more serious problems than you will likely ever confront. You can learn wonderful lessons from them — one of which is the lesson is that you can turn around any negative situation and view it differently. You can reject the negative echoes and fill your chamber with new ones that empower you.

Use your creative mind to work for you, instead of against you. Create an Outlook Makeover for thinking more powerfully and creatively. Replace *What if something bad will happen* with *So what? I'll handle it.* Change *Oh my!* into *Big deal.* Here are several more thoughtful examples of how to craft your interior renovation.

Terribilizing: I feel overwhelmed; I never feel good.

Possibilizing: I've come through problems in the past. I can handle all that comes my way, one step at a time. I choose to see what is right about my life, not only what's wrong. Life is good.

Terribilizing: I'm all alone and will never have another relationship.

Possibilizing: I have some great friends and am open to a new and wonderful relationship. Perhaps it's time to join a group that does something I'm interested in. I can fill my alone time with enjoyable things to do. How I feel is up to me. I love this freedom!

Terribilizing: What if I don't do well on this test?

Possibilizing: All I can do is my best and let the rest follow. I am intelligent and I always give my best effort.

Terribilizing: What if I don't get the promotion? We'll go hungry, lose the house, and have to live on the streets.

Possibilizing: Maybe I'll get the promotion and maybe I won't. Either way, we will be okay.

Terribilizing: Why is Bill so mean to me? I guess something is wrong with me.
Possibilizing: Bill is a decent guy, but this is his problem. I am a caring, loving person, and deserve better treatment than that.

Do you see how the thoughts bouncing around your echo chamber can powerfully influence your thinking? Terribilizing weakens you. Overcoming fear and worry means reassessing your old thinking processes. Empower yourself with possibilities instead of sinking into doom and gloom.

Most people worry about the future; it's natural. But instead, you can focus on the here and now, and develop creative plans for dealing with the worrier in you. Taking small steps to solve your problems, instead of worrying about them, transforms you into a take-charge person who realizes that you have all the power, talent, and resources you need.

Such was the case for Patrice Billings. Upon retiring from twenty-eight years of a very structured work life as a police officer and helicopter pilot, Patrice was worried about what to do next. How do you top an exciting career spent living your dream? She had completed ten years on the SWAT team as a highly trained precision marksman. She was chief pilot and had some incredible experiences, like high-speed criminal chases and assisting the officers on the ground by locating suspects, as she could see things from the air that the ground officers couldn't see. When all that ended at the age of fifty-one, she initially thought, *Gee, this is going to be great. It will be like a permanent vacation. I'll mend the fence, buy a new motorcycle, travel, and maybe write a crime novel loosely based on my life.*

However, home-improvement projects and new toys do not make for a life of significance. Those things can fill time and make one feel busy, but how does one find a new path? After years of flying her police helicopter, Patrice was concerned, and she worried some days that she would not find meaningful work of a different sort at ground level.

Unbeknownst to Patrice, right around the corner from retirement came a business opportunity and a master trainer who would teach her success principles that would guide her from being a retired cop to a professional speaker and published author.

First came a new concept: network marketing — something Patrice never could have dreamed up. She did not like sales, and she didn't have a lot of phone skills. Her experience with building relationships went something like this: "Put your hands behind your back. You're under arrest."

The key ingredients to her transformation were willingness and open-mindedness. These were concepts that were drilled out of her at police academy and during her many years on the force. In law enforcement, willingness means following and abiding by strict laws and procedures. And open-mindedness . . . just try arguing with an officer when you are under arrest.

Patrice was invited to participate in a Mastermind group that met over the phone weekly for twenty-six weeks. She developed relationships with other adults who were seeking a new path and forming their own businesses. She learned how to visualize an abundant life and create a vision board. She learned how to write and recite affirmations and big goals, like owning her own helicopter and having a vacation home in Colorado. She also learned how to make and keep promises to herself, and hold herself accountable for achieving small as well as big milestones.

Since her retirement, Patrice has been published in an anthology called *The Seven Points of Impact* (LFK Consulting, 2011) and is in the process of completing her first novel. She expects to write a series of books about a woman crime solver, loosely based on her life, and is building an international network-marketing business with a health and wellness company. She also envisioned seeing the world, and has now traveled to Mexico, the Netherlands, and the Caribbean, and has been to several places in the United States that she never had time to visit while working a grueling schedule in law enforcement. She is also visualizing and anticipating visiting all fifty states and seeing as many national parks as possible.

The take-home message from Patrice's story is that life is not static; it is dynamic. Many life changes, including retirement, job loss, children leaving home, moving, and so on, can be stressful and seed much worry, terribilizing, and anxiety about the uncertain future. Instead of focusing on your worries, change your outlook to create a vision larger than your current circumstances. By envisioning a new path, you're forging ahead into a more positive and fun future. The key ingredients are being open to many possibilities and being willing to take steps to accomplish your goals.

You choose whether to accept the negative voices in your echo chamber or challenge them with your own newly developing beliefs and CORE powers. Become a creative problem-solver and take the scared you within, who worries "I can't," and turn her or him into a "can doer" who is willing to try.

Chapter Summary

- Much behavior is automatic and based on old thinking habits.
- If you are a worrier, you are also likely to be a highly sensitive person who can quickly feel stressed and overwhelmed.
- When you constantly worry, you become an expert at terribilizing.
- The same mind that turns small problems into major disasters also makes you an imaginative artist, colorful writer, witty

conversationalist, or creative problem-solver.

- Guide your personality to work for you instead of against you by confronting your thinking habits.
- Worriers and terribilizers listen to a mental echo chamber filled with "nots" and "can'ts."
- A mental echo chamber filled with self-limiting ideas drains your power and makes you feel like a helpless victim.
- You always have alternatives. You can choose to possibilize.
- By deciding to possibilize instead of terribilize, you make the choice of power instead of fear.

New Strategies: Power Up and Worry Down

THE PLAN

Examine your current worries and determine how you can possibilize instead of terribilize.

TRY IT

Make three columns:

I am worried about	My thinking is saying	I can possibilize by

153

In the first column, write something that worries you, such as, "I am worried about losing my job." For the second column, you would write what your head is telling you about it, such as, "My thinking is saying, what if I lose my job and go broke?" In the third column, counter that terribilizing thought with a better and more reasonable possibility, such as, "All I can do is be the best employee possible. I will save some money from each paycheck as a backup. I will focus on what I can control, not what I can't. I'm going to be just fine no matter what happens."

Try the same technique with other worry thoughts. Learn to do this first on paper, and then use it when your mind shifts into worry. It is a powerful technique.

POSSIBILIZE

I am powerful. I am capable. I am loving.
I am in charge of my life.
Every day I am getting better at solving my problems.
I can direct my thoughts.
I choose to find wonderful possibilities.
My home is in my belly button.
My safety and security are all within me.

EVALUATE

How did you feel after listing your worries and choosing creative, empowering possibilities? Did you decide this strategy helps you better deal with worries? If not, why not? Did you like the empowering statements? If not, how can you change them?

Note

1. Elaine N. Aron, *The Highly Sensitive Person: How to Thrive When the World Overwhelms You* (New York: Broadway Books, 1997).

6

OUTLOOK MAKEOVER: REDEFINING PERFECTION

Life is what happens to you while
you're busy making other plans.
— John Lennon

Another powerful strategy for changing a
fear-laden mindset and transforming difficulties into opportunities is learning how
to create an Outlook Makeover to spring
yourself from the trap of perfectionism.
Most people would love to live in a perfect
world. In this magnificent place, life is
always fair, all people love you and treat
you kindly, friends are always trustworthy
and supportive, and good things happen but
bad things do not. Oh yes, and you never
make a mistake.

Most of us would run, not walk, to this
world. Everything would be predictable and
pleasant; there would be no need for worry.
Perfection is attractive because it makes us
feel in control and thus more secure; here,

we know what will happen. The problem is that perfection is an illusion.

Magicians are expert illusionists. They appear to pull rabbits out of hats, cut people in half, pull quarters out of ears, and the like. They seem to exert total control over their environment when, in fact, they are simply controlling the audience's perceptions. When we seek to be perfect and try to become magicians of control, we are pursuing a costly illusion because, in reality, we exert very little control over anything except our own thoughts and reactions. The price of our self-imposed illusion is worry and often anxiety about that which we don't, and can't, control. The perfect world always clashes with the real world.

When you try to live by perfect world rules, you unconsciously insist that everything and everybody is predictable and right. You choose to be upset when the unexpected happens or when things don't go as you want. You demand perfection of yourself, as well. When you make a mistake, you think it is a disaster. Unfortunately, when you choose to think this way, you chain yourself to a state of continuing conflict.

To shift out of this mindset, you need to create an Outlook Makeover in which mistakes are not dreadful and where you are not required to be perfect. You can begin to make this change by learning how to productively deal with and accept unexpected twists and turns in life.

Here is a parable that illustrates how perfection isn't always as expected and may be in the eye of the beholder.

A wise old Chinese farmer arose early in the morning to tend his fields and animals. He went to his barn and, in passing his prize stallion's stall, found the animal had broken out and run away. Upon learning of the trouble, the farmer's neighbors came over and said, "What bad luck for your best horse to have run away."

The wise farmer simply replied, "How do you know it is bad luck?"

The next day the stallion returned accompanied by a large herd of horses. Shortly afterward, the farmer's son tried to tame one of the wild horses. When the animal bucked, the young man fell off, broke his leg, and couldn't help his father tend to the farm. When the neighbors came over to visit, they remarked, "What bad luck that your son broke his leg."

Once again the farmer asked them, "How do you know it is bad luck?"

The next week a war broke out between the farmer's village and a neighboring province. The young men were drafted to fight and were sent away. Because of his injury, the farmer's son could not go. Shortly thereafter, the villagers sadly learned that many of the young men of the village had been slain in a furious battle.

This story illustrates how the farmer refused to assume doom and gloom, even though things didn't seem to be perfect. You, too, can apply this thinking by shifting your outlook away from the pursuit of perfection and toward the realization that things are happening as they need to happen. Ultimately, one never knows what is good news or what is bad news. Even when we receive bad news, we can develop a mind frame of quiet acceptance of whatever life throws at us. This means letting go of resistance and allowing other possibilities to unfold. Thus, even when things don't go the way you want or expect, you can choose to be peaceful about it instead of being upset and anxious. From this higher perspective, all things are happening perfectly, even if things aren't themselves perfect.

According to Susan Jeffers, PhD, problems and sorrows offer us powerful opportunities to learn.[1] The more we learn, the more we grow. Even what seems bad can teach us valuable lessons and help us become stronger individuals.

Over twenty years ago, after a self-examination of her breast revealed a mass, Jeffers underwent a mastectomy. As she was lying in her hospital bed after the surgery, she realized she had a choice: she could either say no to the experience and see herself as a victim or she could say yes and make something positive out of it. She chose the latter, and her cancer experience set in motion some wonderful changes in — and insights about — her life. She said, "While none of us understands the Grand Design, we can commit to using all our experiences, good or bad, as the building blocks of a powerful and loving life. Then it is, indeed, all happening perfectly."[2]

Dr. Jeffers suggests that we not deny our fears and our pain but that we simply resolve to ride out the bumps, to handle them as best we can, and then let go, releasing our need to control things. This doesn't mean we should become victims who don't strive to change unpleasant circumstances;

it simply means we should do our best, adopting the mindset of learning from the imperfect and releasing the need to control all things. Even in times of trouble, disappointment, and sadness, we can decide to keep our problems in perspective and not view them as the worst possible disasters. Accepting our difficulties helps us grow and retain authentic power. Shifting perceptions from the need to make all things perfect means:

You can handle whatever happens.

Sometimes, our situations seem too much for us to handle. Even with seemingly insurmountable problems, beneath it all, we have the ability to see things differently and work within those circumstances.

In *Man's Search for Meaning,* Viktor Frankl chronicles his experiences in a concentration camp. Despite the dire circumstances in the camp where his captors stripped Frankl and others of the very essence of their external lives, he remembers those who walked among the huts comforting others and giving away their last piece of bread. From that horrible experience, he searched for a deeper meaning in life and found one. Everything can be taken from a man or a woman but one thing: the ability to choose one's attitude in any given set of circumstances, to choose one's own way. This human freedom can never be taken away.[3]

When you know that the deeper meaning in your life may be revealed by the perfect unraveling of events — including the challenges and mistakes — then you stop expecting life to be perfect in the way you have traditionally defined it. Your problems may not be simple, but their solutions are. You are the only one who can make you happy. You are the only one who can tackle your problems. You are the only one who can choose to see your own life differently. Don't blame others or your circumstances. Dig yourself out of your own rut.

One of the obstacles we frequently face is the fear of making mistakes. When we worry about being perfect, what follows is the absolute dread of committing an error. Perhaps we equate making mistakes with being out of control. We try to be flawless and expect life to return the favor. We fail to understand that success is a journey fraught with trial and error. Instead of worrying about the detours, we can embrace them for the information they provide (e.g., telling us we are going the wrong way and that we should try another). What if mistakes were sometimes beneficial? What if mistakes opened a portal to greater understanding? Would you still dread making mistakes? Theodore Roosevelt, the twenty-sixth president of the United States, said:

"It is hard to fail, but it is worse never to have tried to succeed."

When failure is supplemented with knowledge, it is no longer failure. Many of our most esteemed metaphysical teachers believe our lives have a design and divine purpose — the template by which our spirits learn and evolve; before we ever appear on earth, we have already chosen the circumstances and situations that will occur for us to learn certain lessons. This school of thought suggests that we choose our parents, sexuality, place of birth, race, and so on; we create our circumstances for the purpose of soul learning. This also suggests that our pains, loneliness, disappointments, and even addictions are doorways that can lead to growth and awareness.

You may be saying, "If this is true, what was I thinking when I chose this?" But if our problems are indeed our best teachers, this makes them a rich and fertile soil in which to plant the seeds of self-knowledge.

What can we learn from the problems we face? How can we transform our worries into opportunities for personal and spiritual growth? What if life is a living laboratory?

In science, when you want to understand something, you first develop a hypothesis or idea about how you think something works, and then you set up an experimental design to perform tests and determine if your idea is correct or not. As you conduct the experiment, you write down exactly what you did, noting all that happens, and in the end, you draw conclusions. If successful, you repeat the experiment several times to see if the same things happen again. From there, you design more experiments to test the results in different ways. Finally, you go beyond that and look into it in even greater depth. You expand beyond your initial observations and keep seeking further answers. In science, you're never through, because each level of awareness dissects only one layer of understanding; each is a stepping stone to the next. Discovery emerges slowly by repetition and continually taking small steps into expanding knowledge. Those eureka moments happen only to those who are patient, creative, and perseverant.

In the laboratory, failed experiments can be the greatest teachers. I always emphasize this to my students. I once worked on a project in which I was trying to clone the gene for a protein in the immune system called *membrane cofactor protein*. No matter what I did, I couldn't make the rather archaic, but established, methods work. After weeks of unsuccessfully trying, I buckled at the last failure. I was so upset that I left the lab and went to relax in a nearby park. Sitting on the ground next to an old oak tree, I laid my head against the sun-warmed bark and muttered, "Tree, what should I do? I've tried everything and feel so frustrated!" I closed my eyes and didn't expect an answer. At least I had a good listener to lean against and felt comforted by saying the words out loud.

Later, back at the lab, I tossed all the old reagents. I cleaned up my desk and decided to check my mail slot. As I did so, I noticed an advertising blurb for a new product for exactly what I had been failing at. *Hmm,* I thought, *this sounds interesting. It's supposed to be faster and more efficient. What a coincidence!*

I purchased the new product and it worked the first time. After I mastered the technique, I taught it to others in the lab. They loved it too. The new system became the standard for everyone. "Never underestimate the value of a failed experiment," I always say.

By learning to turn your failures upside down and inside out, you can use them as stepping stones to skip through worry and perfectionism. By asking for help and opening up to it — however it comes — you allow greater insights to enter into your life. Although my first set of experiments didn't seem to be happening perfectly at all, my failures were right on track because they led to something better for me and, ultimately, others.

How about you? Can you remember a situation when something did not happen as you wanted it, yet it redirected you to a better way? Although you may have worried and fretted about the failures, did they end up teaching you a valuable lesson? Most worries are an unnecessary burden because even imperfect circumstances can lead to opportunities for learning and growth.

WABI-SABI SAVVY

Wabi-sabi, a Japanese philosophy, describes beauty as "imperfect, impermanent, and incomplete." It honors all things dented, scratched, weathered, and worn. (Imagine that, you perfectionists!) This view of beauty has evolved over the centuries from early

Buddhist teachings that focus on the transient nature of life and the value of just being. Today, particularly with regard to art, wabi-sabi means "imperfect beauty."

Wabi-sabi brings a quiet acceptance of life as it is, rather than what we demand it to be. It inspires us to look beyond what we see, despite perceived flaws, and seek a greater understanding of the beauty that is all around us. A chipped bowl, old wood, aged fabric, or yellowing paper — all can be objects to celebrate.

There is an exhibit in a Tokyo art museum's wabi-sabi section that showcases a very special treasure. Sitting on a pedestal in a prominent area of the room is an old vase. Shining upon it is a bright spotlight aiming at a very prominent feature: a large crack running straight down its center.

It is important that we develop our own wabi-sabi savvy, to transform our demanding and perfectionistic outlook into a quiet acceptance of the transient but beautiful nature of our own lives. We can begin to experience a peacefulness despite our own "cracks." We can begin to realize, through a quiet acceptance and an inner knowing, that all can be harmonious. We can shine our internal spotlight on celebrating who we are and on the gift of life that is always, in its own way, already perfect and beautiful.

SAYING "OKAY" INSTEAD OF "NO WAY"

When you shift your outlook about what is perfect, you begin to view your difficulties differently. You find creative ways of dealing with them. You empower yourself, dig down, and find the strength you need to handle your problems.

It has been said, "Fear knocked at the door. Faith answered, and no one was there."

Once you see that our lives are shaped and molded by our reactions to what may, on the surface, seem to be imperfect situations, you take a giant leap out of worry and into power. Are you willing to accept and work within your perfectly imperfect world? Are you prepared to develop creative ways of dealing with your problems? Are you willing to consider them as challenges, not victim-producing disasters?

Are you choosing the attitude that you can handle whatever is happening? This frame of mind empowers you and helps break the chains of worried thinking.

The ride may not be smooth, but when you go with the flow instead of against it, you are moving forward. Do your best, change what you can, and after doing that, let it go. With patience and practice, you will become a less worried, more creative, and stronger individual because of the bumps on your road.

Reinhold Niebuhr's Serenity Prayer is so simple and insightful, especially in our work to deal with worry in positive and healthy ways:

"God, grant me the serenity to accept the things I cannot change,
Courage to change the things I can,
And wisdom to know the difference."

It suggests doing your best, improving things where possible, letting it go, and then being peaceful about it. Mistakes can be the pathway to learning. After all, to profit from your mistakes, you've got to go out and make some.

It also helps to keep your sense of humor. The late comedian Dudley Moore said, "I have learned from my mistakes and can repeat them exactly." By developing a tolerance for occasional chaos and grinning at gross imperfection, you flow with life rather than against it. When you release your worries about perfection and control, you are in flow. When you believe that problems can have purposes and provide opportunities for learning and for growth, worry begins to diminish and your resolve strengthens. Whatever happens, you can handle it!

Chapter Summary

- Those of us who worry tend to want everything, including ourselves, to be perfect.
- The illusion of perfectionism always clashes with the real world.
- Things are happening perfectly even when they are not what you think of as perfect.
- You can choose to view your problems and imperfections as opportunities to learn.
- Don't deny fear and pain, but resolve to handle them and then let go.
- It is hard to fail, but it is worse to never have tried.
- Shifting your outlook and redefining perfection means you realize that, to profit from your mistakes, you've got to go out and make some.

New Strategies: Releasing from Perfection
THE PLAN

Are you demanding perfection? Do people and events fail to live up to your expectations? Do you worry that you won't do something perfectly? How does this kind of mindset make you feel? Good, depressed, anxious, angry?

Recognize your choices. What other ways can you think about people acting differently than you want? What other ways can you think about it when something goes wrong? What other ways can you think about something that is stressful?

Try It

What bothered you recently? Write about that in your journal and consider your feelings and thoughts. Ask yourself: Why did I feel this way and what was I demanding of the situation? Now do a rewind. If you released your demand for perfection, how could this have served to help or to foster your growth?

Possibilize

Here are some manifestos to help overcome perfectionism. Develop your own or modify:

I am learning to flow with life.
I am getting better at handling obstacles.
All is well.
I choose to move forward happily and easily.
I am a wonderfully creative problem-solver.

EVALUATE

How can you learn to say "okay" instead of "no way," and flow with your life instead of against it? Can you forgive others as well as yourself for imperfections? Can you find peacefulness in people or situations that appear flawed? Can you see them from a different, more productive standpoint?

Notes

1. Susan Jeffers, *Feel the Fear and Do It Anyway: Dynamic Techniques for Turning Fear, Indecision, and Anger into Power, Action, and Love* (New York: Fawcett Books, 1987). In this book, Dr. Jeffers describes how to transform fear and eliminate negativity, as well as discussing her struggle with cancer.
2. Susan Jeffers, *End the Struggle and Dance with Life* (New York: St. Martin's Griffin, 1996), 76–77.
3. Viktor Frankl, *Man's Search for Meaning* (New York: Washington Square Press, 1984).

7
OUTLOOK MAKEOVER:
BLAME, ANGER, AND GUILT

If you want to awaken all of humanity,
then awaken all of yourself.

If you want to eliminate the suffering in
the world, then eliminate all that is dark
and negative in yourself.

Truly, the greatest gift you have to give is
that of your own transformation.

— Lao Tzu

We often unconsciously carry negative
mental baggage loaded with blame, anger,
and guilt. This chapter shows powerful new
strategies for dealing with these troubling,
worry-provoking emotions, and helps you
create an Outlook Makeover to cultivate an
inner template for recognizing, resolving,
and moving beyond such baggage.

Our lives revolve around our relationships
— intimate relationships, parental relation-

ships, professional relationships, friendships, and so on. These can be a source of great joy, happiness, and fulfillment. But relationships can also lead to great sadness and despair. The challenge we face is to maintain our loving feelings without being pulled into negativity. Achieving this balance is no easy task.

A great and wise master met with Peter, a good man, a curious man, someone who sought enlightenment. The master said to Peter, "Have a seat and a cup of tea. How may I help you?"

Peter replied, "Oh, master, you are so wise, so enlightened. I seek your counsel about something that troubles me."

The master nodded his head and said, "Yes, my son, what is your question?"

Peter looked intently at the wise one and said, "I've been married three times and have had many romantic relationships in my life. They just never seem to work out. What I would like to know is how can I have a wonderful, lasting, loving relationship?"

The master stroked his beard, looked up, looked down, took a deep breath, and said: "What other questions do you have?"

The question of how to have wonderful relationships can vex even our wisest sages and experts. Relationships often challenge us in many ways. When we respond with blame, anger, or guilt, instead of helping our relationships, we create a chasm that separates us from those we love as well as our own feelings of love, contentment, and peace. This is an abyss filled with worry and suffering. Indeed, these negative emotions have physical consequences, such as affecting our hearts. The pause between each heartbeat, as measured on an EKG, provides a glimpse into how we are feeling, according to the Institute of HeartMath. Negative emotions show a more ragged electrical pattern between beats than do peaceful feelings.[1]

Our emotions also affect how we react. When we are in a state of emotional flux, we react more and think less. However, when we focus on peaceful feelings, we respond more productively and can connect to the quieter voice of inner guidance that empowers, nourishes, and creates more harmony. It vetoes worry and instead connects us to a higher realm of communication. In the words of the great Sufi poet Rumi:

"What was said to the rose that made it open was said to me, here in my chest."

Poets and masters teach us that there is a better way than blame, anger, guilt, and the worry that accompanies all three. Our "rose" will never open to reveal its grandeur unless nurtured by loving kindness, compassion, and acceptance. Keeping the gates of this higher energy open and flowing requires us to become aware of the energy we are sending out. Recognizing when we automatically turn on negative reactions will help us find ways to manage and transcend them. When challenges present themselves, take time to consider your responses and choose wisely.

You may hear something like this when you listen to your negative thinking:

BLAME: Whose fault is it, anyway?
It's that person's fault.
It's all my fault.
ANGER: This shouldn't be happening.
Why does this always happen to me?
GUILT: I shouldn't worry so much.
If only I were thinner.
I deserve this difficulty.

Blame, anger, and guilt don't solve your

problems. Instead, they prolong them and, in doing so, allow worry to build. They also seed internal dialogues that make you feel weak and powerless. However, you already have a key that unlocks your baggage so you can dump out the trash. That key is recognizing your ability to react in a different, more productive way. As discussed in chapter 3, you always have a choice in how you respond. When upsets, setbacks, and difficulties swirl around you with the fury of a menacing thunderstorm, you can take charge of the situation and see it differently.

On a warm summer morning a few years ago, I took my then four-year-old granddaughter to the Saint Louis Zoo. Alexis laughed easily and loved to play. I called her Miss Giggles. The vivacious, blond-haired, blue-eyed dynamo had the innocent wisdom of youth.

After we arrived, we hopped onto the merry-go-round. She wanted to ride on the alligator, and I liked the zebra. As we slowly circled side by side, up and down, the pipe organ music played and the lights sparkled.

Next, we walked to see the polar bears. We laughed to see them sprawled on their backs and slowly rolling over to gaze at the gawkers. We shivered as we went through the penguin exhibit that was kept cold for the arctic creatures, the glass walls allowing us to see them scurrying and swimming underwater. Just before we exited, one of the arctic birds shook itself nearby and sprayed me with water. Peering over spotted glasses, I raised my eyebrows and gazed down at Alexis. She sheepishly looked back to see if I might be angry. I smiled and then she chuckled. Everyone around seemed to be enjoying the exhibit and the trip to the zoo.

We went into a pavilion to get balloons painted on Alexis's arm. She proudly displayed the black, red, and blue balloons. As we left to explore another area of the zoo, it began to sprinkle — and then rain poured furiously. We ran for shelter and waited with the rest of the scurrying crowd. Some grumbled while others seemed nonchalant.

"You wanted to come here instead of the Magic House," chided a woman, blaming her husband for the misfortune. He looked away, perhaps out of habit.

"Every time we come to the zoo, it rains," said a young teenage girl angrily to her mother.

It looked like the rain was not going to

stop anytime soon. As I looked around, I noticed that the children's zoo section was within dashing distance. The indoor petting area would be a great place to pass the time, so, putting Alexis on my back, we sprinted to the entrance. A young couple ran toward us from the petting zoo, giggling. Suddenly, both of them simultaneously jumped into a puddle. They joyfully yelped as it splashed to great heights. They were soaked and loving every minute of it as they ran on.

Yes, I thought, rain is fun, actually. So you get wet. So what?

The petting zoo was a great diversion for the first thirty minutes, but soon Alexis became fidgety and it was getting late; I needed to get Alexis back home.

What to do — a soaking rain, no umbrella, a four-year-old, sandals on my feet, and the car in a distant parking lot? It didn't take long to figure it out. I decided we'd just bite the bullet and make a run for it. So, off we went into the rain, Alexis riding piggyback as I jogged to the car.

On the way, I started singing, "Rain, rain, go away, come again another day." This was no easy feat for a middle-aged woman jogging with a child on her back. Alexis happily chimed in and giggled between choruses. There we were, Grammy and Alexis, jogging and singing amid a summer afternoon downpour. It was all so perfect — wet, yes, but just right.

At one point, Alexis's painted balloons began dissolving from the rain and transferring to my sleeve. Concerned she said, "Grammy, my balloons are going on your shirt."

I noticed the black paint on my new yellow shirt. "Well, thank you for giving me your balloons," I said.

She smiled and replied, "You're welcome."

Mercifully for my cardiovascular system, we turned down the last aisle, closing in on the car. Then we saw it: a giant puddle. This was not an ordinary, drizzle type of puddle. This was the kind of puddle that only appears during a summer squall. This was an opportunity. "Shall I jump into the puddle, Alexis?" I asked.

Without hesitation, she gave her approval. We picked up speed and went for it. "Woohoo!" I howled victoriously as Alexis laughed.

Pouring rain and puddles at the zoo could have been a ripe opportunity for blaming, for anger, and for guilt. It was for some. But instead of becoming a disastrous outing with my granddaughter, the day became fun and memorable. There are some slight black paint smudges that remain on the sleeve of my yellow shirt, but every time I look at the dim marks, I smile and remember the good time we had getting it stained.

If you want to jump into your life's puddles, you can. Instead of assigning blame, flow with the course of events. Instead of bolting into anger, find what could be enjoyable. Instead of lapsing into guilt, forgive what seems to be wrong and deal with it. Your reaction is up to you — you have a choice. Recognize that blame, anger, and guilt are caustic cousins. Each leads to focusing on what is wrong. As we worry about the upsetting situation and our possible culpability or role in it, we slump into negative emotions that have no solution.

You can always seek more positive ways of dealing with upsets. Life is what happens while you are busy making other plans. Why worry about detours? Just enjoy moving along the path. Jump into all puddles!

In the words of an anonymous philosopher, "Life isn't about waiting for the storm to pass. It's about learning to dance in the rain."

THE SOLUTION TO BLAMING

People react differently to unpleasant situations. When our plans are interrupted, disappointment and anger are natural emotions. Often, worriers tend to be highly analytical, impatient, and expert faultfinders. We assign fault like a self-righteous judge pounding a gavel and declaring, "Guilty!"

Our brains churn with the energy of constant analysis. We try to figure out whose fault something is and why it happened, and we think about it again and again and again. We dissect every negative event and upsetting situation in an attempt to understand what went wrong and to prevent it from recurring by determining who was at fault. Unfortunately, we can't change the past. Even so, we replay the scene and create ways we could or should have acted. We go around and around, spinning in the same thoughts. But instead of resolving the issue, we only increase the negativity. Blame and guilt don't solve anything.

When we assign fault, we declare internally that all is not right and that it is because of someone's errors. This is our way of analyzing and correcting something negative. It is a strategy that uses available information to make a judgment. We seem to have evolved this mindset as a way to live together in a group. It helps people peacefully coexist. We have rules. We must follow them, and if we don't, we get punished. It helps keep us civilized and helps us avoid the harmful impact of others (or so we think).

Breaking the rules can cause worry and anxiety. We learn this from an early age and hone it in adolescence. For example, fear of social rejection can be especially strong in adolescents who are transitioning to adult society. Gregory S. Berns, MD, PhD, and colleagues performed a behavioral study to better understand the neural and behavioral mechanisms governing social influence.[2] They focused on the music that teenagers decide to purchase. Participants' brains were scanned during the study. The teens listened to music clips, rated how much they liked them, and provided an overall rank. Then they listened a second time with or without being shown the popularity ratings of the music. The study found that teens who hadn't seen how peers rated the music changed their ratings 12 percent of the time. On the other hand, teens who were shown ratings changed 22 percent of the time. Indeed, in 79 percent of cases, the teens changed their likability rating in the direction of the popularity rating. That is, they followed the crowd.

Brain scans of those adolescents who saw that their ratings differed from popular ratings showed an increase in activity in brain regions associated with anxiety. It seems that conforming was motivated from anxiety and the prospect of being "contrarian." Thus, anxious feelings may drive individuals to switch their choices in the direction of social consensus.

But there is an important balance here. We must be able to distinguish between what is needed for peaceful coexistence versus what creates unnecessary personal struggles. When we blame, we are assuming that something is correct and something else is incorrect. These value judgments can be faulty. That's because we are assuming we know the rules and the correct way to do something; that is, we pound the figurative gavel and declare that someone is right and someone is wrong. A more productive strategy is to simply think differently about upsetting situations. We can instead draw on the wisdom of our inner spirit and allow our peaceful, spiritually grounded side to emerge.

Life is not a courtroom. It is a living laboratory. By becoming a student of life instead of a judge, you enhance creativity and learning. By actively experiencing and seeking a higher ground, you proactively create better solutions to problems. You are in control. You run your own experiments. This is not to say others cannot or do not contribute to upsetting situations, but it is *you* who chooses to blame and give away your power to another, or to an event, because you seek fault rather than knowledge.

You set yourself free and begin to heal when you stop finding fault and start dealing with your problems from a higher perspective. How can you do this? The Outlook Makeover for blame is gratitude; adopting an attitude of gratitude replaces faultfinding negativity that only seeds stress and worry. This means changing your attitude in several ways:

• Become a student and learn the lessons.
• Become grateful instead of hateful.
• Become aware of your emotions and thank them for their input.

How do these approaches help overcome a worry-laden mindset? It's because of the way life's energy works. Remember: what you think about expands.

Thus, shifting your mental gears into gratitude gives you latitude, and when you have latitude, you can choose to set your spirit free. That is, it opens up a wonderful new channel where you focus on what you have instead of what you do not have. It focuses on observing your feelings instead of absorbing or denying them. It focuses on responding positively instead of negatively.

Instead of dwelling on fault, begin to solve the problem by placing the emphasis on how you can learn from and overcome the difficulty. Instead of focusing on what's not right, focus on what is or how you can deal with the situation in a more productive way. This allows your energy to draw feelings of strength that counter feelings of fear and powerlessness. Changing the emphasis from blame to gratitude doesn't absolve others of their responsibility; it merely helps you resolve your role in the situation.

Want to have more money? Recognize and be thankful for the money you already have. You have a lot more abundance than many people in the world. Be generous and charitable with your money. This creates an opening that allows more of the same to flow to you. Thus, what you give away boomerangs back to you in other ways. This works with all emotions; when you give away anger, you get *that* back in return as well.

Want to be happier? Avoid blaming and try to grow from the experience. Can you help others because of what you suffered? Can you find some meaning in your pain? Can you excel despite the difficulty?

By changing your outlook from blame to gratitude, you engage in a process of construction rather than destruction. Instead of blaming, choose to see the difficulties in your life as powerful opportunities to grow and to learn.

What feels upsetting to you now? Do you feel isolated because others hurt you? Do you feel like less of a person because you often feel worried and unsettled? Do you feel hopeless and blame others for your predicament? Do you feel that things aren't fair?

Remember, there is no rule of life that declares everything will be easy and fair. If everything were, wouldn't life be rather boring? Stop wasting your energy on blaming; instead, redirect its flow into more positive, powerful, and creative ways of dealing with problems.

What do you feel blocked about now, and what can you do about it? What do you feel passionate about? What do you dream of doing, and why aren't you doing it?

Do you love animals but can't have any? Volunteer at an animal shelter or a vet's office.

Do you wish others would treat you more kindly? Then put out that same energy, for yourself first and then for others; volunteer where you can be in a loving and giving mode, such as at a nursing home, hospital, or school.

Do you feel that you don't have enough money? Take notice of how much you already have, be thankful for it, and strive for what you would like to have. Give to a charity that you feel particularly passionate about.

If you are around negative people, recognize it is their choice and their opportunity for growth and learning. Put up a mental barrier to keep their negative energy away from you. Help where you can without buying into their negativity. They have their own road to travel.

As you interact with others, notice things that you honestly like or appreciate about them. Write a positive note to someone.

Watch the energy grow. But remember, you are not trying to control them; your honesty and heartfelt positive energy simply expand out and will draw more of the same to you. If others respond positively, that's great; if not, it's due to their own inability to allow positive energy into their lives.

As you begin discovering ways to be grateful, you draw more to you that you can be grateful for. It's not always easy to feel grateful, especially if you encounter serious problems.

One month after her wedding day, thirty-three-year-old Cami Walker was diagnosed with multiple sclerosis, a chronic and progressively debilitating illness.[3] Cami somersaulted from feeling as if she were on top of the world with the love of her life to plummeting into a pit of depression, anger, and worry over a life-altering battle with an unseen enemy. Her life had changed nearly overnight. One day she seemed fine. The next day she awakened to weak and tingly hands, and she had lost vision in her right eye.

Overwhelmed, frightened, and in continuous pain, she worried constantly, *I'll end up in a wheelchair, poor and abandoned. My life is over. Why did I get this horrible disease? It's not fair!* As Cami spiraled downward on a path of continuous negativity, her health further deteriorated and she could barely walk.

One day, a friend and spiritual mentor of Cami's gave her an unusual prescription: Give twenty-nine gifts in twenty-nine days. Record what you give in a journal. If you forget a day, start over.

Though skeptical, Cami thought, *What have I got to lose?* She began giving small amounts of money to strangers, lending an ear to a friend who needed to talk, giving flowers to her caretakers or people on the street, providing a good belly rub for her cat, and so on. Each day she wrote what she did in her journal and recorded her experience of giving.

As Cami continued, she quickly noticed that a major shift began taking place in her life. She had stopped focusing on who to blame for her illness and focused instead on giving. She became happier, felt more empowered, and her health improved considerably. She wondered, if it worked for her, could it also help others? She decided to start 29 Gifts, an online twenty-nine-day giving challenge. It quickly grew into a worldwide movement that continues to change lives and give help and hope to thousands of people.

Recognizing and eliminating a blame-loaded mindset and replacing it with generosity and gratitude can open your heart to healing, inner power, and greater peace. Armed with patience and perseverance, adopting an attitude of gratitude empowers you. And when you feel strong and capable, worry fades like a morning shadow in the midday sun.

QUELLING ANGER BY CULTIVATING CLARITY

Anger is an emotion that often accompanies blame. For worriers, anger appears in two varieties. Quick-fire anger happens when you lose your temper or explode into a tirade. Smoldering anger simmers and is sequestered internally, seeding resentfulness, interior hostility, and withdrawal. Anger is a natural emotion; how we deal with it once it happens is a matter of choice.

How do you experience this emotion? Do you explode inside, outside, or both? Do you consider anger bad? Do you feel it is better not to show anger? When you feel anger but don't deal with it, you suppress powerful emotions that will likely surface in other ways.

Further, if you feel things will never get better, you are now adding hopelessness to the fires of anger. Mixing these two can quickly torch your sense of happiness and security, leaving you feeling anxious, worried, and burned out.

Have you grown up feeling that anger is beneath you? Do you think it is necessary to be pleasant and patient all the time or else you won't be loved, respected, or admired? You may have never really learned how to effectively handle anger except to bury and ignore it. This is especially true if you were raised with the mindset that everybody should get along and that you must nurture, not show anger. This may cause you to feel that anger is decidedly unnatural and wrong. If you feel this way, your inner mindset commands you to hold back the dam of your emotions, that they are neither valid nor valuable.

As a teen, I fit this pattern, and I remember occasionally hitting walls, pounding mattresses with my fist, and yelling into pillows. That was actually a healthier response than when, as an adult, I buried my anger. By that time, I was entrenched in the mode of trying to rationalize my way out of anger. When I couldn't and it would erupt, I felt confused as to how to handle it. As a result, when it broke through, often it was out of proportion and very upsetting. Instead of discussing the situation in a calm and clear manner, I was worried, emotionally volatile, and overreactive. Because these emotions were more upsetting than helpful, I became an expert at avoiding anger. However, we cannot trick our natural emotions. My strategy of burying and avoiding anger only resulted in backing me into a corner with a smoldering and insidious form of anger.

The bad news is that anger will not be silenced or buried for long. Anger will surface. When it is not consciously acknowledged, you will feel worried, crabby, resentful, ridiculing, or emotionally flat. If not expressed and dealt with, it can surface in your health too. You can catch the flu, feel sick to your stomach, develop headaches, or have a host of other bodily reactions. Many studies have suggested the powerful impact of emotions on immunity and health. Certainly, the more you worry, the more likely you are to suffer from a variety of medical complications, such as lowered immunity, heart disease, gastrointestinal disorders, headaches, and musculoskeletal pains.[4]

Some chronic worriers have an opposite pattern, always feeling angry and expressing it. They are the fly-off-the-handle types.

Carol, a successful young attorney, fit into this category. She was an angry "overreactor" whose rush of emotions would cause her to explode into tirades that she later regretted. Carol was also a chronic worrier and often unhappy. As she began to seek solutions to help herself improve, she decided to start taking responsibility for her own feelings and reactions instead of blaming others. This required a lot of practice and help, but once she learned how to express her pure and honest emotions in a more balanced way, she felt something new: a feeling of freedom and strength.

It seems we wax and wane in our expressions of anger, depending on our upbringing and individual personalities. Regardless of whether you experience fiery or smoldering anger, the end result is the same: Worry and fear multiply in the fertile soil of anger. If you want to overcome your worry-laden, anxious mindset, you must learn to deal with this very human emotion.

Anger happens because of the conflict between what you *want* and what you *get*. This emotion is providing you with valuable knowledge. Either you need to make changes to better resolve the anger-inciting situation, or you need to change how you are thinking about it. Your inner self may be shouting, "I'm mad as hell and I'm not going to take it anymore!" while your outer self may be shushing that voice, keeping it stifled. In either event, the anger is providing a signal that something is amiss and needs to be dealt with in some way.

What can you do to help resolve anger in a productive way?

• Accept anger as a message.
• Develop a way to calmly handle the situation.
• Be clear in your response.

A great way to do that is to express yourself in "I" messages instead of "You" messages. "I" messages state how *you* feel without blaming the other person or assuming you understand what motivates their behavior.

Here's an example: A friend says something unkind that makes you feel hurt and angry. If you're on autopilot, you might fly off the handle and automatically say, "You're a jerk. Where do you get off saying anything about me?" You might not say anything at all and fall coldly silent. You might think they *meant* to hurt you and feel like it's your fault in some way. In any event, you feel hurt and angry.

There is a more effective way to deal with being upset than yelling or sulking. You can express what you feel and convey your hurt by saying, "When you said I was stupid, *I felt* very hurt. *I'm angry* that someone I care about so much would say something so hurtful to me."

Do you see the difference? In the first instance, you handle your anger by blaming the other person and saying, "You're a jerk" or "I'm not talking to you anymore." Or you blame yourself and feel sad. Those are retaliations that will be responded to negatively or not at all. After all, if you judge something they said with the assumption that you understand their motivation, yet do not reveal how much it hurt you, you are being dishonest with yourself as well as with them, and you are failing to communicate how you truly feel. We often assume that the person with whom we are speaking knows (or should know) how we are feeling, but in reality, they often do not. A more effective way to handle something that hurts you is to express the emotion by saying how the action made you feel — without put-downs.

By using the strategy of "When you . . . , I felt . . . ," you open the door to better communication. Instead of retorting with something hostile or becoming sullen and with-drawn, you communicate your feelings in a more effective way.

It may take several more "I" messages to continue the conversation and resolve the differences, but at least you now have stated what you feel. You have shown yourself that your own feelings are important to you and that you can take care of yourself emotion-ally. That is a healing step for personal empowerment and inner peace. The point is to release your feelings productively, regard-less of whether the person you are speaking to apologizes or responds in a way you want.

Our relationships can be a huge challenge, especially for the highly sensitive personal-ity of the chronic worrier. We often must chart this territory alone, as our parents may not have been helpful role models. In school, though we learn much about his-tory, mathematics, and language, we seldom are given tools for successfully negotiating the intricacies of human interactions. We may fend for ourselves by reverting to our autopilot programming. This can do more harm than good.

Another way to communicate how you feel without alienating the person you care about is to speak from the heart. This doesn't mean sugarcoating your anger;

instead, you enter through a doorway of communication, seeking out a more positive way to express yourself.[5] By paying more attention to how your heart feels, you focus more and draw an experience that increases the feeling of love to you. When you begin to feel negatively during a conversation and have a damaging thought about it, immediately search for an *equally true* thought that makes you feel better to express.

Better listening and communication skills that focus on an open heart can enhance the compassion and connection you feel for the other person. You are not suppressing your feelings, but rather being authentic in sharing what you are thinking and feeling.

"I'M SORRY" MESSAGES

Another type of "I" message is the "I'm Sorry" message. This is a way to acknowledge and better deal with upsetting situations by saying "I'm sorry that . . ." This is not apologizing for your behavior or assessing fault. Rather, "I'm Sorry" messages open a doorway to resolution by allowing you to express heartfelt regret about a situation:

"I'm sorry that we don't agree. I feel sad about this."

"I'm sorry we aren't seeing eye to eye."
"I'm sorry that we are having this conflict."

The key to succeeding with "I" messages and "I'm Sorry" messages is to make them their own reward and *not* a means to control others. After you have taken the time to say "When you . . . , I felt . . ." or "I'm sorry that . . ." do not insist that the other person immediately accept your point of view.

In other words, simply state what you feel and release yourself from the outcome. If the other person apologizes or works with you further to explore the issue, great. If not, just remember the point was for *you* to acknowledge the importance of your feelings and to simply release them in a healing, loving, and effective way, instead of exploding or smoldering. When you can authentically discuss how you feel and release the need for a certain outcome, you also release worry. That's because you recognize that you have done what you can, stated what you can, and realized you can control only your response, not the other person's.

Learning to become assertive requires practice and experimentation. You aren't an expert instantly. But with time and practice, it begins to feel more natural and self-empowering. This helps diminish the powerless feelings generated by fear and worry. Becoming assertive helps you accept and deal with anger. If you're a people-pleaser and feelings-suppressor, you probably haven't spent much time learning this way of taking care of yourself.

"NO" IS NOT A FOUR-LETTER WORD

People cannot read your mind. If you're hurt, you must deal with it. If you really want something, it's okay to ask for it — and to doggedly pursue it. If someone wants something from you, it is okay to say no.

Sometimes saying no can be difficult if you have been programmed to believe you need to help all people, at all times, and consider them first. This presumably charitable attitude is a deceit to your spirit, because you are not following what you believe to be right and good for you. When you become a slave to the wishes of others, it chains you to resentment and consumes your energies. You lose your power and become a helper slave. You give away your power to the people who want you to do something for them. When you say yes to everyone no matter what they ask, you do not necessarily help them either. Life's problems are everyone's opportunities. Are you delaying *their* progress by helping? Could saying no help them more?

When friends or others ask you to do something you would rather not do, there are a few simple strategies for saying a polite no.

You can say no directly: "No, thanks!" or "Nah, I'm not interested."

You can say no while leaving other possibilities open: "I can't stay now, but we could meet later."

Finally, there's always a way out by saying, "I'll think about it." This buys you time to make a decision.

Whatever you say, say it firmly, so it's not misinterpreted. And stick to your guns. You don't need to explain yourself or offer profuse apologies for your decisions. A simple no is quite sufficient.

As worriers, we concern ourselves with how others will respond to our no. In reality, most people will take it in stride. The next time you receive a call from an insistent telemarketer but are not interested, just say, "No, but thanks for the offer." If they come back with programmed reasons for you to reconsider, repeat the phrase. Don't be wishy-washy and begin to hedge or give in to demands for further explanations, which they may then try to refute. Consider it a way to practice nicely saying, "No, thanks."

GUILT WEAKENS, FORGIVENESS EMPOWERS

Guilt is another emotion that can prove useful in the proper context by encouraging you to evaluate your actions. Guilt is your internal judge of your behavior. If you felt good about every action, you would never learn what is okay and what isn't, as you and society define it.

We learn guilt at an early age. It's our first introduction to the world of rules. As little kids we hear, "No, no, that's bad," or even, "No, bad boy" or "No, bad girl." We quickly learn that love or approval is withheld if we do certain things, which makes us feel bad. We learn what not to do, and this imprinting works well to keep us from running out in the street and getting hit by a speeding car. It can help to teach us not to climb on things from which we might fall and hurt ourselves. It teaches us that we can't treat others in certain ways.

A problem arises, however, when guilt is used to control someone in unhelpful ways — that is, when you feel guilty about something that is not really your fault.

Guilt can be a cover-up for low self-esteem. Do you feel bad that you are not the perfect mother, father, son, daughter, or friend? That you don't have enough money? That you can't control your weight, your caffeine intake, your addiction to nicotine? Do you think you have done something wrong if someone isn't nice to you? Low self-esteem and feelings that you don't measure up to your self-imposed standards can lead to chronic worrying.

True guilt helps us change our behavior for the better, such as when we feel bad that we haven't called our mother in a while, or that we haven't been more supportive of a child going through a difficult time, or that we are spending too much time on the internet instead of working at our job. False guilt means giving in to the "shoulda, woulda, coulda" mindset. It means that you blame yourself for failing to meet arbitrary standards you have set or that others have programmed in you. Falling into the "shoulda, woulda, coulda" pit traps you in the unchangeable past, causing you to dwell on:

I *shoulda* done something else.
If only I *woulda* done this instead of that.
If only I *coulda* done better.

The past is a done deal; it's over. The only

thing you can do about the past is to learn from it. You live in the present and go on from here. One way to climb out of the "shoulda, woulda, coulda" pit is to make a plan, chart a course, and take the necessary steps to accomplish your goals. While you can't change the past, you can forge your own future.

If you feel guilty about something you've done or not done, begin to change your point of view by starting with small goals. For example, my fears kept me anchored close to home.

I felt very uncomfortable going too far away. I was also a single parent of younger kids and had a reasonable excuse to stay in the vicinity of my home. I felt guilty not only that I was too anxious to travel but also that I couldn't take my kids on vacation because of my anxious feelings.

I wanted to overcome the fears that were crippling my life, so I decided to practice going farther from my home. I also wanted this to be fun, so I changed my point of view. As children, my brother, David, and I would go exploring around our grandmother's house. When we stayed with her, we would head out to a small creek that wound around the subdivision, following its winding curves and stealthily walking as we explored. We called it Hidden Creek. To add to the mystique, around its final curve lay a mausoleum/cemetery where we heard organ music filling the air. We weren't two kids at their grandmother's for the weekend; we were explorers of a strange new land. I liked that feeling.

I told my kids we would begin some new adventures and go out exploring. They loved the idea. We packed up supplies (food, binoculars, bags for collecting stuff) and on an early Sunday morning headed out to Eureka, Missouri, a small town about forty-five minutes away near the Meramec River. Although I felt shaky and worried at times, I focused on the wonderful feeling of getting out and doing something new and fun. As I practiced feeling "normal" in the situations that caused me worry, I began to feel more normal.

We hiked along the river, and at one point, I saw a rock that interested me and picked it up. I later wrote "Eureka" on it, and it served as an inspiration for healing and a reminder of the joy I felt in successfully challenging myself. My children had a great time exploring. When we came home, I knew that I had begun my journey out of fear. Was traveling forty-five minutes beyond my comfort zone a real victory? You bet. It was a small step, shaky and uncertain. But it was a step.

The philosopher Lao Tzu said, "A journey of a thousand miles begins with a single step." I had a thousand miles yet to go, but I had made that first step — not because I felt that I should do it but because I wanted to do it.

Your power builds and guilt subsides as you progress in small steps toward the goal you've set for yourself. Applaud yourself for each step and continue setting more goals.

Another power-packed strategy to help you unload your worry-inciting feelings of blame, anger, and guilt is to nurture your ability to forgive. Using this Outlook Makeover, instead of dwelling upon how others have wronged you or the mistakes you've made, begin to take back your own power by making the decision to forgive.[6] When you can forgive someone, something, yourself, or just life as it is, you begin healing and empowering yourself. You release the stranglehold of the emotions of blame, anger, and guilt on your life.

Forgiveness doesn't mean that you deny mistakes, approve of someone's vices or selfishness, or banish all pain. Rather, forgiveness focuses your spirit on continuing your life, proceeding with your journey, and releasing the grip that keeps you stuck in pain. When you forgive, you do so under your own power, your own will, and your own choices.

Childhood can be a source of great happiness, fond memories, and at times, much pain. As children, we may not be able to process negative events that impact our lives. Even so, we are not anchored to our past. We have the capacity to better understand and reframe these experiences as adults in a way that helps us, rather than keeping us stuck and attached to the negative experience. By learning to forgive, we release the grip of childhood pain and begin our recovery from its negative impact on our lives.

Linda grew up in a home that often seemed out of control because of her alcoholic father. When she was twelve, her mother divorced her father, and while Linda's connection with him slowly dwindled, she still felt the hurtful effects of her father's emotional abuses. As an adult, she began to understand the role that her difficult childhood had on the worries and fears that plagued her life.

Since Linda could not change the past, she decided she would no longer blame her father or take responsibility for his shortcomings. She decided to release her sadness and anger; She decided to forgive her father. However, by the time she was ready to do so, she found out that he had died six months earlier; she would have no opportunity to meet and forgive him in person.

One day, as she quietly meditated, an image of her father came into her mind's eye. Seeing him as he had appeared in her childhood, she looked him squarely in the eyes and said, "I forgive you." She continued thinking about him and mentally talking to him. "I forgive you for the hurt you caused me and our family. I forgive you for not living up to my expectations. I forgive myself for judging you. I'm sorry you suffered from problems you could not resolve. These were your issues, not mine. I release my sadness, and I release your hold on me forever."

Shortly thereafter, his image disappeared and Linda felt oddly peaceful. She no longer felt uneasy whenever she thought about him, and she realized that she had begun the process of choosing to release herself from the pain. She was the one in charge now, not her struggling, out-of-control, alcoholic parent.

When you forgive, you empower yourself. You recognize and deal with what hurt or upset you. You recognize that we all have our fallibilities and few things are ever perfect. You understand that only *you* can release their hold on you. Once Linda forgave her father, she released the negative grip of those memories on her life. She was the one with power — the power to forgive and go on. When you take charge of your own hurt emotions, their negative influence eventually dissolves. Forgiving does not justify the actions of others; it simply releases their power over you.

Forgiveness cultivates a wonderful sense of peace, power, and tranquility. When you feel at peace, you have no room for feeling worried and anxious. You know you are okay and that you can handle whatever life presents. Inner tranquility grows from self-love and caring. This is the truest gift that you can ever bestow, and it is one you give to yourself.

Chapter Summary
- When we unconsciously carry blame, anger, and guilt, it is a triple whammy for

worry and anxiety.

- Blame is an emotion that seeks to assess wrong by finding fault.
- The antidote for blame is gratitude. Cultivating an attitude of gratitude means focusing on what is right rather than what is wrong.
- Blame is often accompanied by anger.
- One antidote for anger is to resolve issues with "I" messages; these messages state how you feel, not what someone else has done wrong.
- Guilt is a natural emotion designed to help us judge our behavior.
- *True* guilt helps us change our behavior for the better; *false* guilt happens when we allow others or hurtful memories to control us and we give in to the "shoulda, woulda, coulda" mindset.
- The antidote for guilt is forgiving.
- Forgiving does not justify actions; it simply releases the power of a hurtful experience on your life.
- When you are at peace, there is no room for worry.

New Strategies: Building Inner Power
THE PLAN

Are you a faultfinder? Do you automatically judge everyone and everything around you? How might that contribute to your feelings of anxiety and anger?

If you unknowingly carry around blame, anger, and guilt, it will weaken you and create an unsettled mindset. It's time to unload those emotions and concentrate on positive, lighter emotions. It's time to create a new power base. You begin this process by examining how much blame, anger, and guilt you are carrying. Next, you explore how these feelings influence your life and your anxiety. Finally, develop a more productive plan to address and effectively deal with these emotions.

TRY IT

Compare faultfinding with faultless findings with the following exercise.

Make two columns: **"Old Me"** and **"New Me."** On the "Old Me" side, write Blame, Anger, and Guilt. On the "New Me" side, list Gratitude, "I" Messages, and Forgiveness.

Think of examples of how you have unproductively experienced each of the three negative emotions. Now, turn the tables and write how you could have thought about these issues. Instead of blaming, how could you feel grateful? Have you learned or could you learn something from this? Can you share this experience to help others?

Under "Anger," write how you could have expressed your hurt feelings with "I" messages, such as "I am angry because when you _____, I felt _____"; "I feel hurt because when you _____, I felt _____." Also, try an "I am sorry that _____."

For guilt, write how you feel about someone or something and then what you could say to forgive them and release it. Remember, you aren't approving of their actions; you are releasing their power over you. If you have done something you felt was wrong, decide if there is some way to make it right. Consider how you can find a way to forgive yourself and then move beyond the guilt, loosening its grip on your life once and for all.

Remember that you get better as you practice. You don't start out perfect in the process.

POSSIBILIZE

Enjoy how you can better take care of yourself. Create new power messages as you go along:

I immediately recognize, accept, and effectively deal with my emotions.
I am strong and capable.
I am thankful for _____(e.g., health, family, job, friends).
I choose to feel peaceful instead of worried!

EVALUATE

As you practice new strategies, remember to view this process as an experiment in progress. If your practice of saying "I" messages and "I'm Sorry" messages in your daily interactions doesn't turn out the way you want, try a different way. Always feel free to change anything as you go along.

Notes

1. Rollin McCraty, Mike Atkinson, William A. Tiller, Glen Rein, and Alan D. Watkins, "The Effects of Emotions on Short-Term Power Spectrum Analysis of Heart Rate Variability," *American Journal of Cardiology* 76, no. 14 (1995): 1089–1093.

2. Gregory S. Berns, C. Monica Capra, Sara Moore, and Charles Noussair, "Neural Mechanisms of the Influence of Popularity on Adolescent Ratings of Music," *Neuro-image* 49, no. 3, (2010): 2687–2696.

3. Cami Walker, *29 Gifts: How a Month of Giving Can Change Your Life* (Cambridge, MA: DeCapo Lifelong Books, 2009). Cami Walker's full story is described in *29 Gifts,* and tips on how to apply her lessons in your own life can be found on her website: www.29Gifts.org.

4. Edward M. Hallowell, *Worry: Hope and Help for a Common Condition* (New York: Ballantine Books, 1997), 42.

5. Marci Shimoff, *Love for No Reason: 7 Steps to Creating a Life of Unconditional Love* (New York: Free Press, 2010). *Love for No Reason* explores the effects of positive, loving thoughts and offers other ideas on how to pay attention to your heart and more effectively deal with emotion.

6. Mary Hayes-Grieco, *Unconditional Forgiveness: A Simple and Proven Method to Forgive Everyone and Everything* (Hillsboro, OR: Atria Books/Beyond Words, 2011).

■ ■ ■ ■

CORE CONCEPT 3:
RISKING HELPS ME
RECOVER

■ ■ ■ ■

8
RISKING EXPANDS YOUR COMFORT ZONE

To transcend fear, you must be willing to
risk. You must be willing to go beyond
your comfort zone.
— Terry Cole-Whittaker

Have you begun to realize that recovery
from worry is a process of changing from
the inside out? Have you accepted that,
while giant leaps on this path are possible,
smaller steps more consistently get you
there? This chapter continues to show how
you can become your own safety net. Using
these strategies to tame your fears and worries helps to put you back in the driver's
seat of your life. As you begin to master new
ways of thinking and reacting, it is time to
use those skills in the real world and start
doing the things you worried about or
avoided in the past. After all, a parked car
doesn't go anywhere.

CORE concept 3 is:

Risking helps me recover.

Opening and recovering from worry is energizing; it is not a passive process. It means getting out there and using your new skills, rebuilding your feelings of personal empowerment little by little. This could mean learning to stand alone and still feeling strong, letting go of relationships that do more harm than good, or learning to encourage yourself when no one else will do it.

YOU ARE YOUR OWN SAFETY NET

When you accept responsibility for your actions, emotions, and responses, you learn to become more confident in your ability to handle all that life throws at you, and you become your own safety net whenever worries and doubts arise. It's up to you to start anew and live your life on your own terms, beginning now.

When you quit blaming others for your problems, you can manage difficulties more effectively. It doesn't mean you will never worry again in your life. After all, as we've already covered, worry can be a helpful emotion. Rather, the key to helping yourself when worry strikes is to recognize it, evaluate it, and then manage it. All of this adds up to beginning to worry smart, instead of letting worry get the best of you.

In the beginning of this book, you discovered the incredible power of awareness for self-discovery and self-management. Instead of worrying incessantly while trying to avoid problems and stuffing them inside, you deal with them. Hopefully, you have come to realize how stress and unresolved conflict are like little time bombs ready to explode into worry and increased anxiety. The time to defuse the bomb is as soon as you see it.

By opening up your mind to your buried feelings, you declare the importance of you. When you acknowledge how important you are, you become your own best friend, and becoming your own best friend means you always have help.

Taking responsibility for your own needs and actions places you in power. However, taking responsibility doesn't mean being responsible for everything and everybody. Being all things to all people can create unrealistic pressures that seed super stress. Many of us who suffer from worry tend to feel overly responsible for others. On the other hand, we also tend to not take responsibility for our own fear and concerns. We mull; we don't solve.

Kim was always worried about something. It seemed natural and expected. But during a time of mounting life stresses, she developed other fears, such as being in crowds or being stuck in traffic. She worked with a therapist for several years without making any progress. Kim wanted her therapist to wave his magic wand to banish her fears. After all, he was the doctor and she was the patient. You wouldn't perform an appendectomy on yourself, would you? It's the doctor who takes the lead in your healing, right? Wrong.

The fundamental shift from pain to peace occurred only when Kim realized that she was responsible for her own condition and that she was the only one who could make her life better. As she decided to take charge of her own life by dealing with the stresses that were overwhelming her and by challenging her fears, she became a more empowered risktaker. She found, as she charted a new way to better deal with her stresses, that she also challenged her fears and ultimately regained her peace and power.

Taking responsibility for yourself and your choices is incredibly self-empowering. Your life begins anew each day. It is time for you to establish a new plan of action, to set new goals, and to take measured risks by doing things outside your comfort zone.

How much has fear narrowed your comfort zone, and how can you expand it? Create a list of things you would like to do but don't, because you worry about them. Don't put it off or analyze it forever; start small. Ultimately, deciding whether or not to do some thing boils down to just how badly you really want to do it. Are you willing to make the changes needed to get what you want, to feel good again, and to empower yourself? To reprogram your thinking, create Say-So manifestos (and remember to construct them in the present tense). How do you want to feel?

I can take care of myself.
I am talented and insightful.
I am strong and capable.
I am loving and attractive.

Begin to see yourself joyfully *doing* the things you listed. Pack your manifestos with powerful positive emotions. Open up to the idea that these are things in your realm of possibility. *See* it and *believe* it!

Several times a day, see yourself in the scene you create. Begin to bombard your echo chamber with the idea that you can achieve whatever you set your mind to. Be open to the way your dreams manifest in your life.

TACKLING THE UPPER LIMIT THRESHOLD

Sometimes our earnest attempt to overcome worry hits a snag. We just can't seem to move beyond our limitations despite our efforts. Gay Hendricks, PhD, calls this an "upper limit" problem.[1] Each of us has an invisible thermostat that governs our behavior and expectations for what we can or cannot do. These self-imposed limits determine how much love, creativity, and success we allow ourselves to experience. Often this thermostat range is set in our childhood before we are able to evaluate it.

Perhaps we notice disapproval from our mother when we outshine one of our siblings, experience the ire of other students when we excel in school, or learn that we shouldn't express all of our feelings. We quickly decide to keep our talents in check so as not to potentially hurt the feelings of others or upset the status quo. Such misplaced altruism creates limiting beliefs about how much we can and should accomplish. We unconsciously learn to stay within our self-imposed zones and not risk moving beyond them.

What is clear is that once we arrive at our threshold, our powerful inner programming tries to keep us there. At its fundamental level, the upper limit threshold says, "It's not safe to go beyond this zone" or "I'm fundamentally flawed and don't deserve better." As a result of our worries and fears, instead of taking a risk to get something better, we retreat into our familiar, more secure territory. We may be confused and upset that the same old thing keeps happening. What we don't realize is that we have somehow imposed an unconscious barrier to obtaining our desires. We are unconsciously worried and afraid to risk moving beyond our upper limit. But often we are not happy in this zone of restriction. Somewhere within us, in our higher self, we realize we are holding ourselves back. This duality sets in motion conflict between what we want versus what happens to us. When old, limiting beliefs clash with newer programming for positive feelings, only one of them can win.

Christine was an energetic, enthusiastic, hardworking television journalist who was quickly excelling in her career. Starting as a reporter for the early morning news, she was soon promoted to do reporting for the evening news, which had many more viewers. The station decided to start a new daily show that featured uplifting and positive stories. They needed an anchor to host the program. Everyone thought Christine was a shoo-in for the spot — everyone except Christine. She worried that this was too much of a stretch for her; she worried that she wouldn't be able to afford all the new clothes that she would need to buy since she would be in the daily spotlight; she worried it would be too stressful and time-consuming.

When the producer of the new show offered her the job, Christine said she didn't think it was right for her. Fortunately for Christine, the producer thought she might be underselling herself and asked her to think about it. When Christine discussed her concerns and worries with her best friend, Mary, she got another view. Mary mentioned that she had just attended a workshop on how we self-sabotage. We are always better than we think. We hold ourselves back or create circumstances that prevent us from moving forward. Why? Because of an invisible barrier of which we are seldom aware. The barrier is our upper limit set point.

Christine did some soul searching over the weekend and decided that her concerns about clothes, stress, and time were a smokescreen for her worries over whether or not she was good enough for the job. When Monday came, one of her mentors at the station spoke to Christine and said, despite the station interviewing a number of people, Christine's name kept coming up. She suggested ways for Christine to think about the job differently. That is, how much fun it could be to provide heartwarming, positive stories for the viewers. She also suggested strategies Christine could use when applying for the job.

Christine decided to take the leap out of worry and into risk. She applied for the job and got it. And, oh yes, she got a salary increase that was more than enough to help buy those new clothes she would need. People loved her warm and friendly style. She was an instant hit.

The universe does not set limits; we do. That also means we can remove our own barriers.

TAKING A RISK TO BREAK THROUGH EMOTIONAL BARRIERS

Often in our lives, we have multiple set points. Perhaps we are competent risktakers in one area, such as professional life, but in another, such as personal relationships, we have limitations that keep us stuck in worry and mired firmly in our comfort zones.

When Andrew and Kate met, it was kismet. Both felt they had found the love of their life. Shortly thereafter, they married. It was the second marriage for each.

After a few years, however, things went downhill. Andrew became depressed and less communicative. Kate felt angry. They sought help from a counselor. During their first session, the counselor asked Andrew to describe his view of the situation. He said Kate had become boring and passive. Kate shot back and said Andrew had become controlling and refused to communicate his feelings. The counselor asked them about their lives outside of the marriage. Andrew was a highly successful accountant who had progressed to a top position in the company. Kate was just as successful as a designer.

With further discussion, the counselor suggested that both might be experiencing an upper limit problem. Andrew, despite being a whiz at his job, no longer felt challenged. Having reached middle age, he had also begun to worry that life was passing him by, that he'd never become the artist he secretly desired to be or do the fun things he wanted — but he also felt unable to give up his very comfortable livelihood. These feelings were being projected onto Kate. Because of his upper limit set point, Andrew felt powerless to risk making major life changes to accomplish his dreams. Instead, he passively stayed with his boring job and unconsciously began to see Kate — not himself — as the one causing his misery.

The counselor next asked Kate in what way she might not be communicating her intimate feelings to Andrew, which Kate had accused Andrew of doing. Though she was initially resistant to the counselor's questions, Kate thought for a moment, and then began to cry. What she really feared was the loss of Andrew's love. But she knew she could not control his feelings about her. Instead of risking the loss of his love, she clammed up about her feelings of unhappiness in the relationship. She held back her love and exhibited anger and resentfulness at his seeming lack of caring. Kate had reached an upper limit on emotional trust. A loving relationship was wonderful, but on an unconscious level, deeply intimate love was frightening, unsafe, and too risky.

Andrew and Kate now had a decision to make. Having found the core of their underlying marital problems, could they salvage their relationship, or should they divorce and move on? In order to begin the healing process, they each had to create in themselves the feelings that they were seeking from the other. Andrew needed to take steps to become more fulfilled, while Kate needed to learn how to communicate her feelings honestly and effectively.

After more counseling and soul searching, they decided to take the risk to stay together. Both truly loved each other and also recognized how their dysfunctional childhoods caused them to unconsciously set upper limit barriers to attaining greater happiness. Neither had role models for a successful relationship, but each decided to begin by working to embody the qualities that each person wanted from the other. Together, they sought solutions that supported each other's growth. Working together to build a better relationship would also be a wonderful opportunity to learn, even at midlife, how to break free of the past and transcend the upper limits of love.

Lifting the barrier of limitations expands the universe of possibilities, allowing an evolution of consciousness that connects our sources of love, help, and healing in a powerful and palpable way. Thus, taking responsibility for your emotions is your breakthrough from torment to power. You can become the leader of your thoughts, not the follower of your fears. Challenge your issues to deal more effectively with worry, self-doubt, and anger. Experience empowerment rather than restriction. Think about your life and emotions from a higher perspective to give meaning to your struggles. As you step out of your comfort zone, you will fly into freedom.

WORRY REMEDIES THAT WORK

It takes time to chart a new course for how to more productively deal with worries and challenges. It's important to develop a plan that involves a more holistic approach to dealing with worry (i.e., a plan that enlists the power of your mind, body, and spirit).

Your mind helps direct your conscious

choices, your body is the conduit of your emotions, and your spirit seeks to guide you to your highest and best self. When fully integrated, you can sail past your worries.

Runaway worry and fear can quickly launch a chain reaction of physical side effects as your body churns with negative energy. Muscles become stiff and tense. You feel unsettled. This is an inner signal that anxiety is building. Once that happens, it is time to take charge, focus on relaxation, quell turbulent emotions, and keep things in perspective. Because much worry is held within the body, there are several techniques that are useful in learning to quell the pangs of worry and calm the body.

Take a quick assessment. Are the muscles in your shoulders tight? Are you furrowing your brow? What's upsetting you and how can you resolve that? What can you do to restore a sense of calm?

Belly Breathing

When you notice tension in your body, you can consciously relax yourself by beginning a process called belly breathing. This relaxing technique fills your lungs with soothing air, and the slow, deep breathing helps reset your body chemistry and refuel your system with a feeling of calmness.

Temporarily taking control of your breathing pattern has a wonderful relaxing effect. It consciously helps release tension in muscles and sends a signal to the body's interior to feel relaxed, not tense. As your body pays attention to that command, it focuses energy on your requests, not on the automatic stress response of shallow breathing, tightened muscles, and mounting tension. By practicing when you are calm, you can more easily use this technique when you become anxious; breathing is a natural reflex. If you are concerned with your breathing, gently work on yourself in this area.

Begin the belly-breathing process by focusing on your desire to relax. You can mentally say, "I am calm. All is well." Loosen tense muscles in your upper back by moving your shoulders around. Close your eyes if this helps you concentrate. Rub your hands together until they are warm. Place them one over the other, centering them over your navel. Take in a deep, slow breath through your nose and mentally count slowly to four. Breathe deeply until you see your belly rising.

When you reach the peak, briefly hold on to that breath. Make an "O" by pursing your lips, and slowly release the breath to the same counting chant. In your mind, slowly say, "Relax." Feel your shoulders dropping into a more relaxed position. Now, breathe automatically for a few moments (again, very slowly count to four). You can practice this type of relaxation breathing lying down or sitting.

Repeat the process three times. When you are doing this exercise, it sometimes helps to close your eyes and think of something relaxing as well.

To know that you are breathing deeply enough, you need to see your belly rising. That's why this is called belly breathing. So, when you begin this breathing exercise, check that your belly is rising upward. During deep breathing (the relaxing kind), air comes all the way to the bottom of your lungs, pushing out your abdomen.

Another deep breathing practice comes from a type of yoga called Pranayama Yoga. *Prana* is life force energy, and *yama* refers to control or discipline. Here, breath control is also a spiritual practice. In the yogic tradition, proper breathing brings more oxygen to the brain and the blood, and better controls prana. This type of controlled breathing and subsequent enhanced oxygenation not only provides a sense of calm and security but may also improve complexion and cleanse organs by reducing toxins.

The "Sufi Mother's Breath" of Pranayama Yoga involves the following steps:

1. Exhale with a sigh to reset the diaphragm.
2. Breathe in through your nose to the count of seven.
3. Hold your breath briefly.
4. Breathe out through your nose, again counting to seven.
5. Repeat several times to increase the flow of oxygen to your system.

Get Relaxed

When anxious feelings arise, our muscles automatically tighten. They are doing exactly what we are telling them: preparing to fight or flee. Knowing about this automatic pattern can allow you to choose relaxation instead of tension. Practice this as often as you can to learn how to consciously relax your body. Have you ever seen a rag doll? They are cute, but they are floppy, as if always relaxed. When you begin to feel tense or anxious, focus on being like a rag doll and do the following:

1. While sitting, make two fists and place your forearms on each thigh with fists facing up.

2. Take in a breath through your nose and tense your shoulders as you raise them. Hold your breath while you keep your muscles tight for about three seconds.

3. Now, slowly breathe out by pursing your lips (to slow down the breath being exhaled) while dropping your shoulders and letting your hands open and face upward while they remain resting on your thighs.

4. Very gently and slowly, let your head lean forward while feeling the muscles in the back of your neck gently stretch.

5. Slowly raise your head with your eyes closed and take in another deep breath through your nose. Hold your breath while you smile broadly (and *feel* the smile) for about three seconds. As you smile, you can also add an image of something enjoyable and mentally say, "All is well."

6. As you release the air through your nose, feel totally floppy, and stay in this completely relaxed state for a moment. Then wiggle around, shake your hands out to your side, and just try to feel like a rag doll.

7. Repeat this several times, until you feel your body loosening up.

Meridian Tapping

Emotional Freedom Technique (EFT), also called Meridian Tapping Technique (MTT), is an alternative healing approach in an emerging field called energy psychology, which is used to unlock emotional blocks, restore harmonious balance, and turn negative thought patterns into more positive ones. One of the unique features of EFT is its combination of Eastern therapeutic meridian-point acupressure strategies with a traditional Western talk-therapy approach. EFT is used to treat a variety of conditions that range from chronic worry to post-traumatic stress disorder, and even to enhancing sports performance. A host of metaphysical teachers, clinical psychologists, and medical practitioners have given glowing endorsements to EFT, often saying, "Try it on anything!" Although many of the reports are anecdotal, scientific studies to validate the process are underway.

EFT is a form of psychological acupressure that involves repetitively tapping the fingertips over the meridians commonly used in acupuncture while bringing to mind a traumatic or worrisome event. During this circuit of tapping, statements about the emotional block or problem being addressed (see the example on the next page) are added. On subsequent rounds, statements that reframe the problem with a more positive solution may be added.

The idea of the practice is that negative or traumatic emotions create blockages in the body's energy fields. This can contribute to further stress, fear, and physical illness. When painful events happen, energy circuits related to the memories are created in the body. Tapping can help reduce stress and lower cortisol levels. Cortisol is known as the "stress hormone" and under normal circumstances is needed for our fight-or-flight response.

To begin EFT, you briefly recall the specific problem while going through the procedure of gently and repetitively tapping with your fingertips on a sequence of meridian points. The combined effects from voicing the upsetting feeling while creating a more positive replacement by tapping the energy meridians theoretically clears and corrects the "short circuit," the emotional block, from your body's bioenergy system. After just a few rounds of tapping, balance can be restored. Although the memory remains, the associated upsetting or hindering emotions do not.

The EFT meridian points correspond to some of the acupuncture meridians. (EFT points vary depending on which expert you follow.) Here is a common tapping circuit, which one repeats several times: first create a brief statement of the problem, add a self-acceptance statement that you say while using two or three fingers of one hand to tap on an area on the other hand called the karate chop area (corresponding to the side of the hand where one would, for example, do karate chops), and then begin tapping the corresponding meridian points — eyebrow, side of eye, under eye, under nose, under lip (on chin), collarbone, under arm, top of head, and so on. Visit www.whyworrybook.com to see a video explaining this circuit.

Although the technique is easy to learn, performing it with an experienced practitioner may provide the most benefit. Often there are many aspects of a problem that need addressing.[2]

Here is a more detailed example of how to do EFT:

1. **Identify the problem.** Select the problem that you want to address and create a reminder phrase. For example, "I am worried because I feel I have to keep everyone happy and can't say no." Shorten it to a brief reminder phrase, such as "I'm wor-

ried about keeping everyone happy."

2. **Rate your discomfort.** On a scale from zero to ten, rate the level of discomfort that the thought brings you (ten being extreme discomfort).

3. **Create a self-acceptance statement.** The recommended format is as follows: "Even though (fill in problem), I deeply and profoundly love and accept myself." In this case, you're saying, "Even though I feel so much pressure to keep everyone happy and I can't seem to say no, I deeply and completely accept myself."

4. **Tap and say your self-acceptance statement.** Start the process by tapping your fingertips on the side of your hand below the little finger (i.e. karate chop area), while saying your self-acceptance statement several times.

5. **Tap the meridian points.** Next, tap each of the meridian points that correspond to the circuit, from top to bottom, seven times, while saying the reminder phrase. After several rounds, you can also add an affirmation, such as, "It's not my responsibility to keep everyone happy," "I release the need to be perfect," or "I'm letting it all go right now."

Visit the tutorial center at www.EFT Universe.com or www.whyworrybook.com

for free videos on the process and examples of using it on specific problems.

6. **Evaluate.** Reassess the discomfort level. If tapping is working, it should become lower over several trials.

7. **Repeat.** If needed, repeat the process several times until your level of discomfort lessens. If the level is not going down, you may benefit from the help of a professional. There may also be additional aspects of the problem that need to be addressed.[3]

Focus on Now

Managing worry involves the mind, body, and spirit. In addition to all the tools provided earlier, here is a simple, mind-based strategy to consciously slow the tirade of emotions and focus on the here and now. Look around. Remove the focus from worry and exert your power of observation. Lots of other things are going on in the world right now. Look around and see them. Listen to what else is happening. The birds may be chirping. People may be scurrying to and fro.

Ask yourself, "Am I overreacting? Am I okay right now?"

Now, just *slow down.* Focus on the present moment. Don't create catastrophes in your head or languish in the hurts of the past.

Here's a little exercise: Don't think of a pink elephant.

That's easy, isn't it? Just don't think of a pink elephant. Did you see what happened? The first thing you think of is a pink elephant. Thus, when you focus on something you want to avoid, you give it power. Instead, guide yourself to focus on what you *want,* not what you don't want.

When you are in an uneasy situation, look around and focus on the present moment for several minutes. Instead of thinking, "I have to avoid this thing I'm worried about," focus on something else. Notice the interesting things around you, even name the items you see. If you are by yourself, do so out loud. Notice every tiny detail; continue noticing and even naming what you see for five to ten minutes.

Focusing on something other than your tension helps to pass the time until you re-center yourself. Placing your attention on something else can help you stay in the present, instead of terribilizing about the unknown future.

My sister Margie has a favorite saying for when she detects "what ifs" creeping into her thoughts and seeding anxiety: "Keep it real." In other words, when she finds herself terribilizing, she reminds herself to stick to the facts, like the steely detectives from *Dragnet.*

When I detect terribilizing, I might say, "Next channel, please," as if I were holding the remote control and wanted to change what I was viewing on television. This tells my worry chatterbox to switch from that program into something else. I repeat this whenever I lapse back into negative thinking.

What might work for you? Can you develop a phrase to keep your thoughts calm and in the present? Remember, you can't feel relaxed and tense at the same time.

Choose to be relaxed. Remember, you create your world by how you *think.* Your ideas and feelings shape your view and experience of life. What are your ideas and feelings creating? Recognize that you become what you think. Learn to focus your mind on what you want to happen, not what you don't want.

Embrace the Unknown

What do you hear most often as you depart from your friends, family, and cohorts? "Take care" or "Be careful." Obviously, your friends and family care about you and are expressing a desire that you be safe. But the general idea imparted by such phrases is, "Hey, it's dangerous out there. Look out! Keep your head up and watch out for bad stuff."

Unfortunately, this also sends out a message that taking risks could be harmful. Worriers often don't like to take risks because it makes them worry even more. However, building personal power, venturing out into the world, and taking healthy risks are all part of your endeavor to respond to worry in a healthy and positive way. It's time to adopt a different frame of mind such as, "Take a risk," "Try something new," or "Get out there and start doing."

Taking a risk doesn't mean being foolhardy and doing dangerous or stupid things. It does mean trying, exploring, and risking. You can't overcome your worries by wishing. At some crucial time, you must begin venturing out. You must begin to take small steps out of your fears and into the world again.

Start simply by simply starting. Draw a line in the sand and say, "I'm moving on from here. I'm getting over this beginning right now. I refuse to go on this way." You do this by taking small risks and challenging something that you have avoided or about which you have felt uncomfortable.

Then, you gradually empower yourself to do things you thought you could not.

A key element is to make it fun. Don't grit your teeth, clench your fists, and push through your fears while fighting with yourself to do it. Rather, plan to do something that you consider a little scary, but do it because you also think it can be enjoyable. Practice in your imagination first. See yourself doing it and being happy. Create imagery and internal statements about the activity you wish to do. Place power statements on your mirror so that they are the first things you see every morning. This is your internal practice time. See it, believe it, do it!

As I was recovering from anxiety, I had made some great healing strides. I could travel comfortably and had flown extensively. Then came a work conference in New York City. I would be speaking to a national group of scientists about my research relating to smallpox. New York? I had never wanted to go there and considered it a concrete jungle. I worried that it might be unsafe and unfriendly: traffic congestion, tunnels, towering skyscrapers, wall-to-wall people, and so on.

Recognizing my negativity about going

to this unknown territory, I decided to try a different mental approach. Susan Jeffers, PhD, suggests embracing our uncertainties and regarding them as open invitations for learning,[4] so instead of wallowing in negativity and "what if" thinking, I adopted a different attitude and mentally said, "I wonder what I will learn from this trip?" Each time I began to worry, I mentally repeated this question. It quickly counteracted my uncomfortable concerns. By removing my pessimistic internal dialogue, the trip transformed into an adventure that held opportunities to learn something new about myself and the world in which I live.

Luckily, I gave my talk the first day, which allowed time for sightseeing. I went exploring on foot, since I was staying in the heart of Manhattan. Yellow taxis zoomed everywhere. People passed by, speaking all kinds of languages. I strolled past street vendors, shops of every kind, historic buildings, and modern towers. St. Patrick's Cathedral stood tall in its grandeur, Broadway bustled, and the famous Times Square churned with activity and sparkling neon lights. I walked for hours and took it all in. The next day, I ventured to Central Park, an oasis of green amid the skyscrapers. People rode in horse-drawn carriages, had their portraits sketched, and walked their dogs.

I learned that New York held an energy all its own . . . exciting, lively, and even friendly. New York was not scary; it was enchanting. That's what I learned by allowing myself to embrace the unknown. I could have given in to my worries and my fears. Instead, I recognized them, told them I would be fine, and then proceeded to show them resoundingly that the unknown can indeed be fun.

But what if you are about to do something potentially scary, such as undergoing surgery? In this setting, the risks are not voluntary, but nevertheless reflect a challenge that must be dealt with.

My sister Margie chose to embrace the unknown to deal with a hand surgery she needed to correct an injury she incurred at work. Normally Margie carried water and some food, and had tranquilizers available. For surgery, however, she would need to fast the night before. We discussed possible ways for her to take charge of her concerns and doubts.

She knew that her safety props would

245

be unavailable, so she needed some internal ones that would always be there. She developed a plan to deal with the situation by remaining in the present and countering negative thoughts with a realistic belief that all would be fine.

Margie also wondered what she might learn from the experience. When she arrived at the hospital on the day of surgery, she did not dwell on her naturally anxious feelings, but rather focused outside of herself. She affirmed her belief that all would be okay and that she could handle whatever she needed to handle. She spoke with the various people who prepped her for surgery. She noticed all that was happening around her. When she began to feel anxious, she sang a song in her head, which helped direct her thoughts away from the dark side. Margie was prepared for dealing with the uncertainties of surgery; she had a plan. She sailed through the experience without terribilizing. She learned that despite the uncertainties, she could remain safe by connecting with her inner resources. Afterward, she felt empowered, elated, and stronger.

Whether it's a trip, surgery, or whatever, you are capable of dealing with situations that are unpredictable or distressing. Embracing the unknown means going through a challenging experience with an open mind that seeks to learn and grow. Taking a risk, whether chosen or compelled, and changing your perspective helps elevate you into a higher consciousness of learning from life's experiences. This offers you a chance to push back the barriers of limitations, and empowers you to handle not just some but all the uncertainties of your life.

Three Simple Steps to Stop the Grip of Anxiety

Chronic worrying can keep you tense, on high alert, and lead to anxiety attacks. When stresses become more challenging, you can help yourself by using the "Stop, Look, and Listen" technique to quickly regain the reins of control.

Step 1: STOP. First, recognize and accept that the feeling is anxiety. Next, take charge of your breathing and immediately begin to breathe slowly and deliberately. Remember the belly breathing? This is the time to do it because it can help reverse your body chemistry and restore calm.

Now, stop the runaway train of emotion. You can consciously veto maintaining the fight-or-flight response. Acknowledge the worry but recognize that, in this case, any fear is merely a False Emotion Appearing Real.

Step 2: LOOK. Don't try to control or fight your symptoms. Accept them and remain determined that you are going to ride them out. True power over your worries comes from learning to accept the feeling and not letting it move beyond the initial fear response. Remember, "Fear knocked at the door. Faith answered, and no one was there."

Move around if at all possible, and look around you. Focus on the external, rather than the internal sensations. Ground yourself by focusing on your feet and legs, and gradually move up your body with progressive relaxation. Keep in the now by looking at the details of life around you. What are people wearing? What are the interesting details of your surroundings? Can you speak or joke with someone? Take five full minutes to name things you see. If you find your vision is disturbed, focus on your breathing instead to help restore the normal biochemistry of your body that is thrown off by shallow, anxious breathing.

Step 3: LISTEN. Talk calmly to reassure yourself. Say your power phrases: "Okay, I feel afraid, but that's all right. I can handle this. Am I in a truly dangerous situation? No, I'm not. I simply refuse to fuel these fires. I'm okay. I'm done with this. I have choices here. I refuse this response. I am totally safe and I am okay. In fact, I am a coping machine. My safety is in my own belly button. I refuse to do this."

You can also create and carry cards with your power phrases. They can be phrased as if they were something you would say to a scared child. How would you comfort her or him? You can trust yourself. You really can.

When I was overcoming anxiety, I practiced driving farther distances from home. I feared being away from the supposed safety of my home. Because of that, I mostly stayed within a comfortable distance so that I could get back home if I started feeling anxious. As I was working on changing myself inside, I planned small trips. I practiced mentally to prepare. I envisioned how I wanted to feel. I saw myself doing it enjoyably. I also looked at maps and found different routes. Finally, I started driving. If I started to feel uncomfortable, I would launch into the Stop, Look, and Listen technique. To stay in touch with the present moment and connect with people, I stopped at stores or roadside stands. I briefly chatted with people and practiced feeling comfortable. I listened to audio books while driving, which helped me focus on something other than my churning fear. I brought along water and snacks. As I kept practicing, my anxiety began to lessen.

As you begin to face your fears little by little, your comfort zone expands. The more you practice, the more you build on your successes. Sometimes you may stumble in your practice and skip it or cut it short. Each time that happens, you may feel bad. But you must learn to continue challenging yourself despite setbacks, to forgive yourself for *not* being perfect, and to remain committed to trying and rebuilding.

General George S. Patton said, "Success is how high you bounce after you've hit bottom." An important key for recovery from fear and worry is to practice, practice,

practice, with patience and perseverance. When you want to get better at anything, you must practice at it. If you want to learn piano, you play it regularly and try to improve. If you hit a clinker, you start over or go on. When you practice hitting a baseball, sometimes you don't connect and you strike out. It happens. But you keep at it. Babe Ruth struck out more times than anyone in baseball — but he also led the American League in home runs for twelve seasons.

As you begin measured risktaking, applaud yourself for trying. The point is to get going and to set small, realistic goals. Small successes are wonderful stepping stones. Build on them. When you feel you haven't succeeded with a goal, keep at it.

Thomas Edison experienced nearly two thousand failures when perfecting the light bulb. When he finally succeeded, someone asked if he felt bad that he had so many failures. He quickly replied that he absolutely did not feel bad at all. He had simply discovered two thousand ways not to make a light bulb.[5]

Take responsibility for turning your own negatives into positives. When your frame of mind is to learn rather than to be perfect, failures can be wonderful teachers and motivators. Be gentle on yourself as you begin taking risks. It is easier to sit back and hope than it is to go out and do. It is easier to plan than it is to experience, but risk is a part of life and an opportunity to grow beyond your worries and fears.

Remember, you do not have to go it alone if you are still uncomfortable challenging your fears. Consider working with a therapist who specializes in anxiety treatment. However, it is important to understand that pushing through your worries provides the reinforcement and energy you need to overcome them. You may stumble and fall, but each time you get up and go on, you are moving beyond worry and into more peace and power.

Eleanor Roosevelt was the First Lady of the United States during World War II, when the nation mobilized after Pearl Harbor and battled in many areas of the world. She understood real fear when she said the following:

"You gain strength, courage, and confidence by every experience in which you really stop to look fear in the face. . . . The danger lies in refusing to face the fear, in not daring to come to grips with it. . . . You must do the thing you think you cannot do."

Chapter Summary

- Taking responsibility for moving beyond your comfort zone is self-empowering.
- Healing from worry and fear begins when you are willing to take small risks to expand your comfort zone.
- Learn to relax your body by belly breathing and progressive muscle relaxation.
- Practicing regularly focuses your energies on getting better.
- Even your failures can be powerful motivators for improving.
- To break the grip of worry, remember three simple strategies: Stop, Look, and Listen.
- You can do the things you think you cannot do by learning how to relax when dealing with stress and by taking healthy risks to expand beyond the illusion of your limitations.
- Start simply by simply starting!

New Strategies: If It's Gonna Be, It's Up to Me

THE PLAN

What would you do if you could do anything you wanted? What are you avoiding? You

253

can do the things you think you can't do, by breaking them down into smaller steps. Taking small steps into recovery will help you achieve giant leaps later.

TRY IT

Start with a smaller goal that would be a step toward reaching an even larger adventure. Choose something you want to do as opposed to something you feel you should. Make a plan to tackle it by yourself or with a supportive friend. Choose something that could be fun. Choose a day when you will take a step to begin to do what you want in some way. No matter how small the step, do something that moves your energy toward your goal.

- **Possibilize.** Take some quiet time and possibilize about what you want to accomplish each day. See yourself doing it, enjoying it, and feeling strong and capable. Add strong positive emotions to the scene. Create dynamic, empowering manifestos to say before and during this activity.
- **Plan.** Become more familiar with what you want to do. Do you want to change jobs or start your own business? Find out all you can about the business you are interested in pursuing. If you want to chal-

lenge a fear, such as crossing over bridges, find out about them and how they are constructed. The internet is a wonderful source of information about almost anything. The more familiar something is, the less worrisome or frightening it becomes. Make cards with your favorite positive statements. What works for you? You can trust yourself; you really can.

- **Permit.** If you are challenging a fear, give yourself permission to conclude the activity and continue it later. Outs are simply ways of mentally releasing some of the steam. They are some of the "so whats" to your "what ifs." Applaud yourself for whatever you did to accomplish your dreams.
- **Practice.** If you begin to feel anxious, remember: Stop, Look, and Listen.

POSSIBILIZE

All is well.
I can take care of myself.
I feel completely safe and wonderfully happy wherever I am.
My home is in my belly button.
My strength is within me and my spirit is free.

EVALUATE

As you focus on taking steps to accomplish your dreams, see yourself becoming more self-confident. Support each and every effort. Applaud your progress and forgive yourself when you don't accomplish what you planned. Simply try again. Keep possibilizing and walking into your dreams, step by step.

Notes

1. Gay Hendricks, *The Big Leap: Conquer Your Hidden Fear and Take Life to the Next Level* (New York: Harper One, 2009). Hendricks provides a simple and effective way to overcome our barriers to happiness and fulfillment by recognizing how we unconsciously impose limitations on our own life and how we can consciously reprogram our responses.
2. David Feinstein, "Energy Psychology: A Review of the Preliminary Evidence," *Psychotherapy: Theory, Research, Practice, Training* 45, no. 2 (2008):199–213. A comprehensive review of the scientific literature supporting therapeutic use of energy psychology methods.
3. Nick Ortner, *The Tapping Solution: The Revolution Starts Within* (Newtown, CT:

The Tapping Solution, 2009), 90 min. This movie shows real-life examples of meridian tapping. For more information on meridian tapping, see Patricia Carrington, *Discover the Power of Meridian Tapping,* with an introduction by Nick Ortner (Bethel, CT: Try It Productions, 2008). See also eft.mercola.com, www.eftuniverse.com, and www.whyworrybook.com.

4. Susan Jeffers, *Feel the Fear and Do It Anyway: Dynamic Techniques for Turning Fear, Indecision, and Anger into Power, Action, and Love* (New York: Fawcett Books, 1987).

5. Matthew Josephson, *Edison: A Biography* (New York: Wiley, 1992).

■ ■ ■ ■

CORE Concept 4:
I Embrace
My Spirit

■ ■ ■ ■

9
EMBRACING YOUR SPIRIT: DOORWAY TO HEALING

There are only two ways to live your life.
One is as though nothing is a miracle.
The other is as though everything is a
    miracle.

— Albert Einstein

Lasting healing from the negative effects of worry proceeds from the inside out, empowered by a deeper connection to your spirit. This not only helps you overcome your worries and fears but also can transform your life into one of purpose, power, and joy. Here is the fourth and final CORE concept:

I embrace my spirit.

Embracing your inner spirit and your intuitive side allows you to surge beyond limitations and head into a remarkable realm. In this quiet space, there is no need for chronic worrying. In this quiet space, you are safe and protected. In this quiet space, you are nurtured, loved, and powerful.

TRANSCENDING WORRY, TRANSFORMING YOUR LIFE

As the connection to your spirit grows, you begin guiding your life away from the voice that says "Don't" and amplifying the one that says "Do!" Practice creates energy, and energy fuels your journey along the path of discovery and enlightenment. In time, you can transcend your worries and transform your life. You will no longer need their message. It will be an outdated template that allowed you to develop knowledge and connect to your spirit. Once you reconnect to this unfailing source of power and love, you recognize an inner sense of knowing and strength that some call intuition. But you have to listen for it. That's because fear shouts, while intuition whispers.

Fear rules by scaring you away from things; intuition quietly directs you to follow that which is best for your spirit. As you learn to silence the continuously chattering negative voice, you will begin shifting away from inner dialogues that restrict instead of expand your life. By becoming more selective in the thoughts you heed, something wonderful begins to happen: the portal to your intuition opens up and allows you to hear that peaceful, quiet voice again.

Worry can mangle self-trust and intuition. How can you trust what you think and feel when you feel bad so often? Worry seeds more worry, whereas intuition expands your power beyond physical limitation. As you begin to eliminate your focus on worry, you can also begin to reconnect to your inner sources of guidance. Focusing on love and positive energy amplifies them and displaces fear. This doesn't happen overnight. It's like a muscle weakened from lack of use. But as you practice at living less in your head and more in your heartfelt intuitions, you strengthen that connection and allow help and guidance to come through.

Pierre Teilhard de Chardin, a French philosopher, Jesuit priest, and scientist, said, "We are not human beings having a spiritual experience. We are spiritual beings having a human experience."

Call it what you will — Spirit, Universe, Higher Power, Universal Energy, Great Spirit, Mother Nature, God, Divine Providence, or Grace — tapping into this energy moves us beyond our ordinary lives and into a connectedness with all that is, was, or will be.

Sacred beliefs come from many different

traditions: Buddhist, Christian, Jewish, Hindu, Muslim, and so on. Some people don't connect through formal faiths, yet they still experience a sense of oneness and reverence for being alive. Although the outer wrappings differ, they all share the belief in something beyond what our eyes see and what our ears hear. Embracing that "something" invites an even stronger connection, further energizing our journey away from fear and worry.

SCIENCE AND SPIRIT

The worlds of science and spirit have long been immiscible, like oil and water. However, a new trend toward connecting the two has been gaining momentum in recent years. Slowly permeating the scientific realm are new studies, especially by quantum physicists, demonstrating states of other consciousness and energy that can be measured and studied. What is emerging is a picture of how we are connected in an expansive universe of interacting energies.

For example, Andrew Newberg, MD, director of research for the Jefferson-Myrna Brind Center of Integrative Medicine at Thomas Jefferson University Hospital and Medical College, is one of the pioneers in an emerging field called neurotheology, which studies the relationship between the brain and religious experience. As part of his scientific studies, Newberg performed brain scans on Buddhist priests and Franciscan nuns during prayerful meditation. He compared their scanned patterns before and during meditation and found that, during deep meditation, the neural activity of the parietal region of the brain sharply decreased.

The parietal region of the brain is involved in orientating us in space and time, as well as providing our sense of self. The decreased neural activity after meditating, compared to before the subjects went into meditation, is consistent with the subjects' reported experience of oneness. The emerging theory is that deep meditation alters our perceptions of the physical limits of the body. When this happens, our sense of separateness disappears. The brain no longer supports the view of boundaries between the self and the outside world. Instead we begin to perceive the self as endless and connected to everyone and everything. This is the experience of oneness.[1]

Lynne McTaggart's groundbreaking book *The Field* describes new scientific discoveries supporting the existence of oneness.[2] Physicists have found a quantum sea of energy that connects all of matter. It is teeming with subatomic particles that oscillate between the states of particle and wave. These subatomic denizens transmit energy and information that blur ideas of separateness. This provides a possible mechanism to help explain how, even on a subatomic level, we could be connected. In essence, consciousness is linked to behavior in the quantum world, where all things are connected.

Take the case of the random number generator experiments conducted by the Institute of Noetic Sciences.[3] Their Global Consciousness Project's (GCP) international team of scientists and engineers hypothesized that, when human thoughts and emotions become coherent and synchronized, it influences the behavior of random systems. Thus, they distributed random number generators around the globe and measured the output from the devices. They compared the data with the occurrence of emotionally charged, widespread world events or focused attention by large groups of people. In one example, the GCP found anomalies hours and days before the September 11, 2001, attacks in New York City. In another example, the random number generators displayed variations near the time of the Japanese earthquake and tsunami on March 11, 2011, which persisted to the end of the event. Even events such as the funeral of Princess Diana showed an effect. The data collection and analysis continues.

From a conceptual standpoint, is it a stretch of the imagination to consider our oneness and connectedness? The internet, which enables instant access to information and the ability to interface with people around the globe, is a major source of connectivity. Consider the wonder of being able to pick up a cell phone while driving in the desert of the United States and calling and instantly speaking to a person in England. Connectedness! Think about how much of our DNA scaffold we share with other animals and even worms and plants. Oneness is not such a stretch of the imagination.

THE MAGIC OF COINCIDENCE
Science aside, many of us have seen glimpses of something larger at work; this happens during those moments when we feel a part of something bigger, something loving, something that might even bring us to tears. We know, not just hope, how precious life is and how we connect to it all.

As the American novelist and poet Alice Walker wrote in *The Color Purple,* "One day when I was sitting quiet . . . it come to me: that feeling of being part of everything, not separate at all. I knew that if I cut a tree, my arm would bleed."

Isn't that beautiful? Even if we cannot fully explain it, the sense of oneness can be supremely healing. This dynamic, sustaining inner power is accessible for help anytime, anywhere. Ask for its guidance and it will appear. Ask for help and it will arrive. Ask for transformation and it will occur. Perhaps these things will appear differently than you imagine, but they will manifest in a way that best guides your life's journey.

Unfurling and enlarging your connection to the spirit transforms the ordinary into the extraordinary. You surge beyond limitations and head into the remarkable. A sign that the process is working for you occurs when coincidences begin to appear in your life.

The language of inner connection
is coincidence.

Louis Pasteur said this in a different way:

"Chance favors the prepared mind."

The idea is that we see only when our minds are ready to comprehend. We've all had those "wow, that's weird" kind of moments. Maybe you were thinking about someone and he called you that night. Maybe you were struggling with an issue when suddenly a book dropped off the shelf in the bookstore and it was exactly what you needed to read. Maybe you were wondering how to fix something at home when you decided to turn on the television and up popped a home-improvement show on the subject.

Coincidences can represent a direct pipeline to our spiritual side and connectedness. It's like a mathematical formula in which Coincidences = Cooperating Incidents.

In the field of mathematics, a coincident angle occurs when one line directly connects with another. This can happen in our own lives, when coincidences begin showing up that help direct us to a new path. This concept was termed "synchronicity" by the eminent psychiatrist Carl Jung. He believed synchronicities demonstrate how we are connected with other people and the universal consciousness that he termed the "collective unconscious."

Thus, coincidences or synchronicities may represent opened portals to a domain of connectedness. Tapping into this energy helps propel us along our destinies and offers us opportunities to align with spiritual help and guidance. Recognizing such signs invites more of them into our life.

In my own life, I noticed how coincidences kept occurring as I began making breakthroughs to overcome anxiety. I began keeping track of these in a journal. I called it my meta-moments journal because these occurrences often bridged the gap between the physical and the nonphysical, i.e., the realm of the metaphysical. In this domain, we lump together all those happenings that we cannot explain. This is the arena of faith.

Although our ancestors discovered fire by rubbing sticks together, they could not explain it. They could not yet appreciate that fire simply derives from combustible material plus oxygen molecules — a simple equation by today's standards. They had neither the language nor the necessary insights to understand yet. Still, fire was a transforming accomplishment, even if it was not fully comprehended.

We are the modern cave dwellers of the spirit. We do not know the science that accompanies such metaphysical happenings as coincidences, miracles, and perceptions beyond the senses. We do not even have language for it, much less ways to measure, quantify, and analyze it. Albert Einstein reportedly said,

"The intuitive mind is a sacred gift and the rational mind is a faithful servant."

I wanted to better understand this sacred gift — as well as my connection to my spirit and the universe in which I lived — so I began to study metaphysics. Fear made me feel small and isolated, but I knew inside that I was much more; I just couldn't access it yet. I attended classes on metaphysics, read books, and drove to the lab each day while listening to recordings from teachers such as Wayne Dyer, Joan Borysenko, Christiane Northrup, Deepak Chopra, Caroline Myss, Marianne Williamson, and others. I practiced quietly relaxing and meditating. I opened myself to guidance and projected my own images of healing from anxiety. I felt a new sense of peace and inner strength begin to emerge.

Curious coincidences began happening regularly. I was sitting at a stoplight one morning on the way to the lab and noticed the car in front of me had a license plate that said "ASK," followed by the usual three random numbers. For some reason it stuck in my mind, probably because the three random letters made a word. I progressed a couple of miles farther and then found myself behind a different car that also had the plates beginning with the same three letters. On my way home that night, this time on the highway, I saw another car with ASK.

Wow, that's weird, I thought. *What's the chance of seeing that many plates with the same three letters in an area the size of metropolitan Saint Louis? Interesting co-incidence?* Almost every day for the next several months, as I traveled the fifteen-mile journey to and from work, I noticed different cars with ASK plates. Although the numbers varied, the word kept appearing around me.

I began to expect them and smiled when they appeared. It felt like someone greeted me each time it happened. I chuckled and thought, *What in the world does that mean?* I decided to answer the question myself by determining what my heart sensed from these coincidences. What was the *feeling* that occurred each time I saw such a plate? As I focused within, I knew that every time I saw an ASK plate, it felt like a message of "ask and you will receive." That is, if I wanted something to happen in my life, I could simply ask for it. I could focus on it and invite help. As I thought about it further, the ASK message suggested recognizing my feelings and then doing something about them.

Yes, I thought, *asking implies that I recognize I want something to happen and that I can attract the connection to make it so.* I felt important and deserving. I realized that what I wanted most was to be free from the chains of worry.

After that, when I saw my ASK plates, I would quietly invite further connections. Each time I would say, "I ask for help and guidance to overcome anxiety and grow spiritually." ASK was my mantra and my prayer, and I always followed the experience by adding a thank you.

I continued to see the plates for a long time, and I don't remember when I stopped seeing them. I probably got the message and no longer needed to be reminded. The cooperating incidents helped me embrace my spirit and enlist it in my recovery. I felt a growing sense of inner connectedness, safety, and spiritual power.

But I also knew that the healing came from doing, not just wishing. I knew that even if my initial actions were small, it would get my energy moving away from the inertia of fear.

Fork in the Road

In retrospect, I can see now that I was approaching a significant fork in the road. I didn't know it at the time, but I was connecting to inner sources of wisdom and guidance that would help me make some of the most important decisions of my life. I found that as I asked for help, it appeared in many forms and ways I never anticipated. I learned that spirit touches us in simple and sublime ways.

But I also learned that we must develop a discriminating ear. One day, as I headed into the lab, I backed out of my driveway and noticed that the parking brake light was on. I automatically looked to see if I had released the parking brake, but the brake was released. I hadn't forgotten it. I began to worry. Was it locked up or not? I certainly didn't want to head into work, a fifteen-mile drive, with the car's parking brake engaged. Also, I didn't want to get stuck somewhere. Then, the light went out. I decided it would be okay to drive to work.

Halfway home that evening, the light went on again. I thought, *Is this a sign from the universe? Am I not releasing my spiritual park-*

ing brake? Am I holding myself back? I had learned to look for symbols as well as coincidences. I pulled the car over, turned it off, and pulled up the parking brake. I started the car and then released the brake. The parking brake light was still on. *How could the brake be on,* I mused, *when I can drive the car and it does not feel sluggish?* I decided to continue driving but stop by the dealer to see if the infernal thing was engaged or not. As I described the problem to the service man (minus the potential spiritual implications), he asked, "Have you checked your brake fluid?"

Apparently, when the parking brake light goes on it is a signal from the car — not God — that it needs brake fluid. *Ahh,* I thought. *Good lesson.* Apparently, my training in the metaphysical needed to build some discrimination. Learning to do so required time and patience.

How can we know when something is just a coincidence — or something more meaningful? The best way is to enlist the full help of your mind, body, and spirit. Ask yourself if there is a *feeling* that accompanies the coincidence. The coincidence is more significant to me when I have a feeling about it, rather than merely intellectualizing or analyzing it. See if you feel the coincidence energetically somewhere in your body. Ask the feeling what it means and consider any thoughts that arise. Ultimately, if the experience has significance for your life, your spirit will already know. Then it is just a matter of following your heart and allowing life to play out as it needs to for your highest good.

Jason, a college student, went shopping for clothes with his friend Bobby at a shopping center they seldom went to. Jason found a shirt he liked at an Old Navy store in the complex. As he went up to the checkout counter, his eyes popped and his jaw dropped. The young lady ringing up the sale was the most beautiful girl he had ever seen. Because of the long line, he just took his clothes, thanked the cashier, and headed back to the fraternity house. On the way back, he thought, *Wow, that was one beautiful girl!* As he got out of the car, the first person he met was his fraternity brother Tom, who was heading to work. As they greeted each other, Jason mentioned and described this fabulous girl that he had just met but hadn't asked out.

"Wait a minute," Tom said. "I think that's Melissa. She's one of my girlfriend's best friends. I bet she can invite Melissa up for the party here next Saturday."

What are the chances of this happening? Jason thought. Sometime later, Melissa did attend the party, met Jason, and the attraction was mutual. They later married and three daughters have graced the planet, all because of an amazing coincidence that steered them into their destiny.

Many of us worry about whether we will ever find the right person or that magical relationship. We try our best and do what we can to find "the one." That can certainly help, but sometimes all we may need to do is worry less and pay more attention to coincidences. Paying attention to the message of a coincidence may help steer us into the direction of our life path.

We are all integral members of the quantum soup, the collective unconscious, as well as spiritual beings living here on earth. Our experiences are bathed in all kinds of energies, some known, some unknown. Our connections are myriad. We have the capability to manifest our intentions in some mysterious, undefined way into the physical realm. While we await future studies by physicists to someday provide scientific explanations for these phenomena, the basic idea is that there is much yet to be uncovered in the expanses of science, spirit, and their intimate connections.

Ultimately, the how and why of a coincidence is less important than the realization that we are all connected, that our experiences can guide us toward greater understanding, and that our lives have meaning and purpose.

As we place our attention on building the connection to our spirit, an invisible portal opens that allows the energy of creation to enter our lives. It all begins by focusing our attention on our desire to connect more with our higher spirit. There are many ways to do this: studying masters in the field, attending a spiritual community of like-minded people, and learning to glean spiritual guidance as we go within during meditation. There are many avenues to enhance this inner connection. The more we invite such experiences, the stronger the bond to our spiritual side becomes.

Cooperating incidents may not necessarily appear as lightning bolts or incredible miracles, but if we open our inner eyes to the subtle hues of spirit, we can experience delicate changes in our perceptions that can reveal helpful information, paths of renewal, and pillars of support. Coincidences can provide the quiet miracles and everyday tools that help, encourage, and guide us along the path of love and enlightenment. In this higher place, there is no room for fear.

Chapter Summary

- Long-lasting healing from chronic worrying is empowered by a deeper connection to our spirit.
- "We are not human beings having a spiritual experience. We are spiritual beings having a human experience." (de Chardin)
- Coincidences are cooperating incidents or signs that align you with your intentions.
- Coincidences can open channels of information, renewal, and support.
- Our spiritual connections manifest in many ways.
- When you ask, you will receive.

New Strategies: What's the Message?
THE PLAN
Connect to inner guidance and coincidences. Do your coincidences hold messages for you?

TRY IT

Take time to relax and feel peaceful. Silently ask for the highest sources of help. You can be specific, general, or entirely open. Ask for ways to strengthen your connection to your spirit. Be grateful for the good things you already have. Be thankful for your many blessings. Then, for the next few weeks, keep track of coincidences. Write an entry in your journal. How did it feel when you experienced it: funny, nice, helpful? After you begin to notice coincidences, ask for more help and continued guidance — and always for your highest benefit. As you experience help, express gratitude for it. Be open to how it manifests. Don't make demands about how you want help and don't tear experiences apart with analysis. Simply build that connection, learn to evaluate, and continue to expand outward. Ask and you shall receive. There's more help available to you than you realize.

POSSIBILIZE

I am grateful for help and guidance for my highest good.
I can ask for what I want.
I am strong and powerful.
I am happy, healthy, and loving.

I am calm, confident, and connected to spirit.

EVALUATE

Do you like thinking this way? Are you open to possibilities? Continue exploring and experimenting with how you can best connect and embrace your inner spirit. Release yourself from the need to demand a specific outcome.

Notes

1. Andrew B. Newberg, *How God Changes Changes Your Brain: Breakthrough Findings from a Leading Neuroscientist* (New York: Ballantine Books, 2010); *Principles of Neurotheology* (London, UK: Ashgate Publishing, 2010).
2. Lynne McTaggart, *The Field: The Quest for the Secret Force of the Universe* (New York: Harper Element, 2003).
3. The Institute of Noetic Sciences began the Global Consciousness Project in 1998 as a way to assess the effects of global consciousness in a measurable way. See http://noosphere.princeton.edu/.

■ ■ ■ ■

PUTTING IT ALL
TOGETHER

■ ■ ■ ■

10
CHANGING YOUR LIFE:
CO-CREATING YOUR FUTURE

> Every moment of your life is infinitely
> creative and the universe is endlessly
> bountiful. Just put forth a clear enough
> request and everything your heart truly
> desires must come to you.
>
> — Shakti Gawain

What do you desire for your life? What
would you like to change? Where would you
like to go?

As you begin to more deeply evaluate
these important questions, perhaps it's time
to adopt the mindset of an explorer. Exploration can rejuvenate your sense of enthusiasm and excitement for living. While worry
contracts energy, exploration pushes energy
outward.

When you pursue your passions, the
streaming energy carries you along and connects you with all that is necessary to fulfill
your dreams. Becoming an explorer helps

you to find your purpose, create blueprints, and launch into a new destiny.

Don't worry if you don't feel like an explorer yet. Give yourself some time and consider this: great explorers are usually ordinary people who have an extraordinary trait — passion. Explorers have a burning desire to delve into something that fascinates them. They are both compelled and excited enough to take risks when tackling their goals. Not all voyages of discovery need to be so dramatic and challenging. The journey to fully embrace who you are, reconnect with your spirit, and follow your bliss energizes you to a level above the ordinary.

If you have been using the tools in this book, you have already begun to incorporate manifestos into your daily life. These strong, positive, and purposeful statements are part of the blueprint for recovery. By eliminating the negative chatter unconsciously wired into your thinking, you rewire circuits to respond in a more positive way. Remember, what you think about expands.

Often, what happens in our lives and the directions we take seem like a matter of chance. As you have learned in this book, however, we *can* change our lives by rewiring how we think and react. In this way, we fully cooperate with the forces of creation to become active participants in the co-creation of our future. By placing our thoughts and intentions on what we want, see, and believe, we take an active role in how our lives unfold. Circumstances may not be exactly as we envision, but life will fill in the details to align with our intentions.

To co-create what you want in your life, first develop an image of it in your mind. Then, focus on that idea regularly: See yourself doing it, *feel* what it would be like to do it, and *become* fully immersed in the picture. A key to succeeding with this process is to add strong emotions to fuel your images with powerful manifesting energy. Learning to create something in your mind first allows you to accomplish anything safely and to build your sense of security. By focusing on what you want and seeing it as real, you open the portals of creation.

If you are imagining an object, see yourself holding it, admiring it, feeling happy about it. If it is a situation, see yourself in it, feeling happy and joyful. If it is a state of being, feel yourself acting and being that way, reveling in joy and peace.

Here are a couple examples of how this

has worked in my own life to help combat fear as well as to create what I want.

One of the problems I had for many years was my fear of going too far from home. I mistakenly assumed that if I were home, I'd be safe. In actuality, I was as worried at home as away. So I began to create mental changes. I would close my eyes while relaxing in a comfortable chair. I would silently and slowly say, "I love to travel, to go to new places, to see new things, and I am wonderfully comfortable wherever I go. My home is in my belly button, and my safety and security are all within me."

I could believe this statement because I used to love traveling. In my mind, it was still fun. That is what I wanted to create again. I wanted to be free of my nice, safe, comfortable prison. I wanted to be free to go wherever I wanted and have fun doing it.

I pictured myself in a variety of settings over time. I imagined boarding an airplane and feeling excited. I thought of the flight as my magic carpet ride. I imagined sitting on the beach. I could feel the warm sun shining on me and penetrating my skin. I heard the ocean's soft, rhythmic waves and the chattering seagulls in the distance. Other times, I gazed at beautiful outdoor scenes.

About a year after my recovery, I went to Hilton Head Island for a family Thanksgiving get-together. I arrived late in the evening. The next morning, as I descended the stairs of the rented vacation home and looked around, I was shocked; it was just as I had pictured it in one of my visualizations. The fireplace, couch, tables, and chairs were exactly where I had mentally placed them in my imaginary vacation room. The walls were where I had placed them. The far wall was composed entirely of a set of windows that overlooked the ocean, just as I had seen them. I couldn't believe my eyes. I hadn't locked in any time or a specific place in my earlier manifesto. I hadn't said, "Next Thanksgiving I will go to Hilton Head Island and stay in a cottage on a beach that looks out over the Atlantic Ocean." Rather, I had just crafted the images and felt the joy of being in that place in my mind. In this way, I attracted what I had consistently imagined.

As you focus your intentions to create positive changes in your life, you will see the magnificent unfolding of your dreams. I had envisioned many things. Most of the other ocean scenes also happened in their own time, when I was ready to travel. I have now frolicked in the waves of the Atlantic and Pacific Oceans. I have joyfully crossed the magnificent Golden Gate Bridge in San Francisco. I have hiked in the glorious Red Rock Canyon in Nevada. I have soaked up the sun on the beaches of the exotic Caribbean. Best of all, I have journeyed to Greece, walked among the ancient ruins of the Parthenon, and floated in the warm, beautiful arms of the steely blue Mediterranean Sea. Not bad for someone who was too fraught with worry and fear to even drive to the shopping mall.

Many of us, including you, have stories to tell and inspiring lessons to share. Our road to overcoming the worries that plague our lives may not be a straight and quick path. What differentiates those of us who make changes to improve our lives from those who stay stuck is simply a quiet determination to excel beyond limiting circumstances, and a faith that somehow, in some way, we can do so.

Now is your time to step away from worry into peace, power, and purpose by synthesizing the ideas in this book and formulating them in your own ways to help yourself. It is time for you to put the full force of your dreams into creating your life anew. Remember that your two most powerful tools in this journey are awareness and choice.

You cannot improve something that you are unaware of. You cannot remove your boundaries and soar beyond them unless you see where you have set them. Your invisible prison has been constructed and is maintained in your own mind. See it and understand why it developed. Go within yourself to your CORE power. Choose wisdom over worry. Choose freedom over fear. Choose passion over despair.

You are never trapped by anyone or any circumstance as long as you recognize, accept, and use the power of your mind and spirit. Your path may not be smooth, direct, or uneventful. The journey through worry may challenge your resolve and tax your energies, but this trip is worth the time and effort.

GO FORWARD

Your difficulties provide compelling lessons that teach you about yourself, your spirit, and your world. You can do the things you believe you cannot. Even when challenges seem to be overwhelming and the voice of worry and fear is loud, you can choose to move beyond your circumstances.

The inspiring story of John Tyler Dossett and his family teaches us how to persevere and create a better life despite what seem to be overwhelming challenges.

John Tyler Dossett is a talented artist and an incredible philanthropist who gives all of his earnings to charity. He has one other amazing feature: he's a quadriplegic, except for the ability to slightly move his right arm. Despite his physical limitations, he mixes colors, shapes, and forms on canvas to create vivid sunsets, sunrises, and anything that catches his artistic eye.

The thirty-seven-year-old has a debilitating genetic illness called Lesch-Nyhan syndrome, which strikes in early childhood. For the more than one million children afflicted, a faulty gene passes from mother to son, resulting in a missing enzyme vital for breaking down uric acid. Without it, half of the sons inheriting the mutation develop the disease and suffer from kidney stones, gout, spasticity, self-mutilation, and general weakness. Many die before the age of eighteen. John has defied the odds.

He often wears a Superman shirt. His hero is the late Christopher Reeve, who played the part in several movies, but whose tragic horseback-riding accident left him a quadriplegic and confined to a wheelchair. Like Christopher Reeve, John says he can walk, run, and fly in his dreams.

When awake, however, it is a different story. His parents, Terry and Muffy, along with his nurse companions, take care of his everyday needs. His sister, Aimee, also provides moral support and serves as business manager. To translate how he sees the world into his works of art, John has one requirement: that the handles of brushes, or other objects he uses, be large and easy to grasp. Once in hand, each brushstroke releases a powerful vision that knows not the bounds of the human body. An angel floats in and out of pink and white swirls, a face barely visible in a painting called *Angel of Hope*. The passionate hues of orange and red meet mid-canvas in strong strokes of the brush in another, called *Autumn Stand*. "Go forward," he says slowly, with only half a tongue to help him form the exact words (the other half had to be surgically removed).

John says he wants to do what heroes do: help others. He uses his time and talent to do that. He does not see the mangled body of disability but the beauty of dreams and images. He does not see the tragedy of circumstances, but the opportunity to give back. John has already donated more than $60,000 to charities such as the Christopher and Dana Reeve Foundation and the American Cancer Society's Relay for Life. Although his future is far from certain, John plans to continue taking classes at a nearby college and expressing himself in his art. "Go forward," he says. "Go forward."

Limitations are what you allow them to become. They are the barriers of your own mind. Even in the worst circumstances, there are opportunities to explore, connect, and inspire. Heroes arise from many circumstances — not all dramatic. A hero lives within us all if we care to explore and reach out to that quality. Quiet heroes, like John, show us how to persist, carry on, and excel beyond our fear. In the realm of mind and spirit, there are no limitations.

What about you? Why not begin this process of exploration and healing by creating a new view of what you want for your life? You can't become what you don't dream about. But you can create changes by first deciding to do so. You can create changes by taking that first step. You can create changes by unleashing the power of your inner spirit.

You may take some tumbles along the way, but by getting up with dogged determination and defiantly continuing your journey, you move forward. It takes time to heal from an injury and it takes time to move past negative reactions and the habit of worry. Crafting images first in your mind helps align your energies of creation.

The best way is to start simply and be consistent. Play with it. Have fun with it! Remember that patience, perseverance, and practice propel you forward and engage the manifesting gears of the universe.

As you create your new blueprints for a happier, more fun, and more fulfilling life, you begin to live your life on purpose — not accidentally in worry.

Bertice Berry, a motivational speaker and writer, says, "When you walk with purpose, you collide with destiny."

Remember that, ultimately, your thoughts create your destiny. Walking with purpose means that you direct your life, instead of feebly following your fear. Creating the life you want first in your mind's eye heals and frees you from the inside and dissolves the limitations of worry and fear. Becoming an explorer allows you to find your purpose and your destiny. Enthusiasm and passion replace worry and anxiety.

When you can say, "I am an explorer," you have reached the point in your recovery where you begin to walk with purpose. You *know* all is well. Your world is safe because of your ability to choose. You are aligned with your spirit and purpose. You are free at last.

Ultimately, your worry is your teacher. Learn the lessons and move on. That's what life is all about. Experience and understand; experiment and learn. You will have many challenges beyond your worries, as life is fraught with them, but your struggles give you wonderful opportunities.

As you move past these struggles, you unleash your true power. As you tackle your worries and fears and embrace your challenges, you help others do the same. That is your gift to the world. Whether it is to your children, your partner, your spouse, or your friends, you can stand as a beacon of hope to others who may be struggling. Your growth helps others grow, and overcoming your pain helps others overcome theirs.

The choice is yours. Will you continue the journey? Will you make changes in your own life? Will you overcome your worries and show others that they can too? Will you step into the new consciousness of your own spirit?

Do not impose time limits on your journey, for it will progress at its own pace. Be patient, but persevere. Be gentle and supportive of yourself. And most importantly: practice, practice, practice.

Once you unfurl your wings and begin to fly into your life, remember the words of Mae West: "Too much of a good thing can be wonderful!"

Lift your wings and fly — for you can do the things you think you cannot. Become the leader of your thoughts, not the follower of your fears. This is not the end; this is your beginning.

Chapter Summary
- Exploration pushes energy outward, while fear contracts it.
- To co-create what you want in your life, you must first explore your passions and then develop a blueprint for your mind.
- When you walk with purpose, you collide with destiny.
- Your world is safe for your dreams because

you are aligned with your spirit and purpose.
- Limitations are what you make them.
- You can do the things you think you cannot.

New Strategies: The Five List
THE PLAN
Learn how to focus your intentions and co-
create your life. Align your inner spirit with
your destiny. Renew your enthusiasm for
living the life you want. Develop your own
manifestos and create a Five List.

TRY IT
Generate a list of five positive statements
about how you want your life to be or things
that you would like to happen. Maybe you
would like to own your own company.
Perhaps you'd like to attract the perfect
mate. Use dynamic words and craft it as if
what you want is present already. Relax your
body and take time to develop these images. See yourself doing or feeling what you
imagine. Do this with strong positive feelings and emotions. Change your scene until
it feels right. Practice daily and be open to
how and when your list manifests. There
are many ways for that feeling to come to
you.

POSSIBILIZE

Here are some examples of manifesting statements:

I am strong and powerful.
I feel completely safe wherever I go.
I love traveling, going to new places, seeing new things.
My home is in my belly button.
I attract a wonderful relationship into my life.
I immediately recognize, accept, and effectively address my feelings.
I am fit; I am trim; I am wonderfully healthy.
My relationship with my family is loving and fun.
My job is satisfying, fun, and pays great.
I always have more than enough money to provide for my family, to get what I want and need, and to help others.

EVALUATE

As you draw your attention to your intentions, does it help you feel differently about your life? Do you feel enthusiastic? Do you see yourself and feel the emotions of each statement? Are you open to how your intentions manifest in your life? Are you practicing regularly? Keep trying, be patient, and take one step at a time. Exploring is fun!

ACKNOWLEDGMENTS

I have been blessed to have this book reviewed and endorsed by some powerful figures in the world of healing and recovery. I appreciate their time, efforts, and encouragement.

Christiane Northrup, MD, is internationally known for her empowering approach to women's health and wellness. A noted author, media personality, and visionary, she is a leading proponent of medicine and healing that acknowledges the unity of the mind and body. See her website (www .drnorthrup.com) and wonderful bestselling books (e.g., *Women's Bodies, Women's Wisdom*).

Carol North, MD, is a shining star and national expert in the field of disaster mental health. Dr. North was called to New York City to provide her expertise in the days following the terrorist attacks of September 11, 2001, and to Louisiana in the days following Hurricane Katrina. Dr. North is also a woman who has overcome and lived to tell about her own psychiatric illness. She is a great example of how we can use our own experiences to help and inspire others.

Cathy Turner's life is an amazing story. She overcame suicidal depression and battled for a place on the US Olympic team. She is one of only three people ever to win gold medals in consecutive Winter Olympic Games and ranks fourth for the most medals ever won by a Winter Olympian. Also thank you to **Susan Jeffers, PhD**, and **C. Alec Pollard, PhD**, for reviewing my work.

This book also wouldn't have been possible without the love, help, and eternal encouragement of my wonderful sisters, **Margie Collins**, **Debbie Schnuriger**, and **Linda Lowe** and my mother, **Margaret Myers**. For the great joy they add to my life, I thank my daughter, **Julie**, and my son, **Jason**, and his family (wife **Melissa** and the grandest grand-girls, **Alexis**, **Abby**, and **Samantha**). **Pam Cornwell**, who is not only my treasured friend but was a wonderful support during my recovery from anxiety; and **Sandy Freeman**, who has offered lifelong friendship, support, and amaretto sours.

I also appreciate the help of fabulous book coach and friend **Linda Nash**, as well as my great book helpers from *Anxiety Rescue*, **Sue Sylvia** and **Christine Frank**. In addition, I acknowledge **John P. Atkinson, MD**; **Andree Wallgren**; **Howard Johnson**; and **Michael Dawdy**, for all their support.

Finally, I wish to warmly thank the entire staff of Beyond Words Publishing. Working with them has been friendly, efficient, and fun. I appreciated early discussions with president and editor in chief, Cynthia Black, and with Dan Frost, who gave me the opportunity to prepare this work. I also acknowledge publisher Richard Cohn, Lindsay S. Brown, Gretchen Stelter, Anna Noak, and Emily Han, among others.

APPENDIX A:
QUICK HELP FOR
ANXIETY ATTACKS

If you experience anxious feelings, try these quick coping techniques to help you sail through a crisis moment. Moving past worry and anxiety takes time. Having a plan of action empowers you and reduces feelings of helplessness.

Personalize the following list and add others that work for you.

1. **Slowly say an affirmation.** Here's one example: "I am safe and I am fine. All is well."
2. **Breathe . . . breathe . . . breathe . . .** If your heart is racing, you can help yourself quickly and simply by launching into relaxing belly breathing. Take three slow deep breaths, and watch your belly rise as you do so.
3. **Stop scaring yourself.** Silence that inner chatterbox. Ask, "Am I

overreacting?" Remember to stay in the moment and stop the scary thoughts. Say or think the word "stop."

4. **Relax.** Walk around. Move as much as possible. Swing your arms around or pretend you are hitting a punching bag.

5. **Eat a healthy snack.** Low blood sugar can mimic or exaggerate anxious feelings.

6. **Take an anxiety medication.** Don't feel you have to go it alone. You are working on your skills and you'll become less reliant upon medications over time. Follow your doctor's advice concerning which medications to take, when, and how.

7. **Find something to laugh about or induce anger.** Recognize that you cannot feel two *competing* emotions at the same time. Watch or read something humorous. Sing!

8. **If you are anxious at night, turn on the lights or step outside.** Stargazing can have a very settling effect. During the day, go outside and listen to the birds, connect with nature, walk barefoot in the grass,

water your flowers, and so on.

9. **Comfort your EARL side as you would a scared little child.** Say empowering phrases:

I am strong and powerful.
I can take care of myself.
I am the leader of my thoughts, not the follower of my fears.
I am home wherever I am.
My safety and my security are within me.
I'm going to be okay.
This too shall pass.

APPENDIX B:
BOUNCING BACK
FROM ANXIETY

Consider what may have led to anxious feelings instead of ridiculing yourself. Anxiety is an SOS released by your spirit. It is a call to action and an internal safety valve to help you care for and nurture yourself. Unresolved conflict seeds continual stress. It's time to tackle your issues.

1. **Do an emotional inventory:**

Am I taking care of myself?
Am I attending to my own needs?
Am I using the ideas in the book?
Am I getting the right type and amounts of nutrients?
Is hypoglycemia mimicking anxiety?
Am I having too much caffeine or nicotine or both?
Am I tackling or avoiding my problems?

Am I exercising or using relaxation techniques?

2. **Take time out and pamper yourself:**

Take a warm, relaxing bath with scented salts.
Use lavender or other aromatherapy.
Light candles and play music.
Take the day off.
Visit a park or botanical garden.
Play with a pet.
Do something nurturing and energizing.

3. **Empower yourself:**

Organize a closet, your kitchen, or the garage.
Work (play) in the garden.
Find a puddle and jump in it!

Treat yourself with as much kindness as you would show a child who has had a difficult time. You are worth it! Comforting, pampering, and taking care of yourself helps to quell the calamities generated by your EARL side. Becoming peaceful, focused, and serene calms the pangs of apprehension. When there is peace, there is no need for fear.

APPENDIX C
WHAT IF I NEED MORE HELP?

Here are some helpful professional organizations that can offer additional assistance:

American Psychiatric Association: www.psych.org and www.healthyminds.org

American Psychological Association: www.apa.org

Anxiety and Depression Association of America: www.adaa.org

Association for Behavioral and Cognitive Therapies: www.abct.org

Freedom From Fear (a mental health advocacy organization): www.freedomfromfear.org

Institute of HeartMath (a nonprofit health research and education organization): www.heartmath.org

Mental Health America (formerly National Mental Health Association): www.mentalhealthamerica.net

National Institute of Mental Health: www.nimh.nih.gov

And here are some experts in the fields of self-help, spirituality, and personal growth:

Caroline Myss: Medical intuitive, healer, and bestselling author who lectures and writes on body-mind-spiritual healing; www.myss.com

Christiane Northrup, MD: Internationally recognized, bestselling author especially known for her empowering approach to women's health and wellness. Books include: *Women's Bodies, Women's Wisdom; The Wisdom of Menopause; Mother-Daughter Wisdom;* www.drnorthrup.com

Deepak Chopra, MD: Bestselling author and co-founder of the Chopra Center for Well-Being; www.chopra .com

Edward M. Hallowell, MD: Author of *Worry: Hope and Help for a Common Condition,* which offers great, practical examples and advice from a compassionate physician; www.drhallowell .com

Michael Bernard Beckwith: Spiritual leader and director of the Agape International Spiritual Center. His books include *Spiritual Liberation;* www.agape live.com

Robert L. Leahy, PhD: Author of *The Worry Cure,* which offers practical, easy-to-understand advice and techniques; http://www.cognitivetherapy nyc.com/Dr-Leahy.aspx

Susan Jeffers, PhD: Internationally known therapist and bestselling author whose books include: *Feel the Fear and Do It Anyway* (first published in 1987 and now as a 25th anniversary edition), *Embracing Uncertainty,* and *End the Struggle and Dance with Life;* www .susanjeffers.com

Wayne Dyer, PhD: Bestselling author and one of the most widely known and respected people in the field of self-empowerment and spirituality. His books include: *The Power of Intention, There's a Spiritual Solution to Every Problem,* and *Manifest Your Destiny;* www.drwaynedyer.com

ABOUT THE AUTHOR

Kathryn Tristan has published articles in *PARADE* and *Psychology Today* as well as 120 articles in leading health publications, under her professional name, Liszweksi. She is a member of the Anxiety Disorders Association of America and the American Association of Immunologists, and is on the faculty at Washington University School of Medicine in St. Louis, Missouri.

The employees of Thorndike Press hope you have enjoyed this Large Print book. All our Thorndike, Wheeler, and Kennebec Large Print titles are designed for easy reading, and all our books are made to last. Other Thorndike Press Large Print books are available at your library, through selected bookstores, or directly from us.

For information about titles, please call:
  (800) 223-1244

or visit our Web site at:
  http://gale.cengage.com/thorndike

To share your comments, please write:
  Publisher
  Thorndike Press
  10 Water St., Suite 310
  Waterville, ME 04901